Our Values

Our Values

Stories and Wisdom

DALE EVANS ROGERS
with
CAROLE C. CARLSON

SPIRE

Published by Fleming H. Revell
a division of Baker Book House Company
P.O. Box 6287, Grand Rapids, MI 49516-6287

New Spire edition 1998

Printed in the United States of America

Library of Congress Cataloging-in-Publication Data

Rogers, Dale Evans.
   Our values : stories and wisdom / Dale Evans Rogers with
Carole Carlson.
      p.   cm.
   Includes bibliographical references.
   ISBN 0-8007-1734-1 (cloth)
   1. United States—History—Religious aspects—Christianity. 2. United
States—Moral conditions. 3. Christian ethics. 4. Conduct of life. 5.
Christian life. 6. Rogers, Dale Evans. 7. Rogers, Roy, 1911– . 8. Values. I.
Carlson, Carole C. II. Title.
BR526.R645   1997
277.3—dc20   96-29293

Contents

Preface   7

1. Who Buried America's Values?   11
2. Value of Our American Heritage   23
3. Is Truth Dead?   33
4. My Search for Life's Values   43
5. Value of Tough Times   61
6. Family Values in a Fractured World   73
7. Value of Friendships   89
8. Value of Discipline   103
9. Value of Patience   115
10. A Call to Valor   129
11. God, Give Us Another Chance   139

Notes   149

Preface

Dust filtered into the cluttered office as carpenters shouted instructions over the din of hammers and saws. A major renovation was underway at Roy Rogers' Museum. Dale sat in Roy's brown leather chair, undisturbed by the surrounding confusion. Her son Dusty, business manager of the Rogers' enterprises, and her daughter Cheryl, museum director, stopped briefly to ask her opinion or comment, "Workin' on another book, Mom?" Grandson Dave brought coffee in Styrofoam cups, and great-grandson Dustin came in to get keys and move our cars out of the workmen's path.

Working with Dale is an adventure. Whether we're ducking out of the crowds in an airport, dodging cables and cameras in a television studio, or warming in her memorabilia-filled kitchen, there's a sense of being with a woman who has experienced a lifetime of trials and triumphs.

Dale Evans Rogers belies her eighty-three years. When she walks through a restaurant, heads turn and strangers stop to say, "Hi," as if she were an old friend. (It's mostly those over fifty who recognize her.) Roy and Dale have been known all over the world for their Christian testimony. They have never been reticent to "preach the word . . . in season and out of season," no matter what the consequences.

However, today Dale is angry. Not angry-mad, but angry-disturbed.

"What has happened to America's values?" she asked with new seriousness, looking at me across Roy's desk as if I could give her the answers. "Y' know what I mean?" she said in that probing way a mother does when one of the kids needs to repeat what was just said.

So Dale began to define where she stands on the truly important values. The dictionary defines them as "the social principles, goals, or standards held or accepted by an individual, class, or society." *Who or what establishes America's values?* This is the question we must answer, or as Dale says without subtlety, "We will die."

With Dale supplying the core of the ideas and me filling in a little research and providing a few comments, we began this project and discovered in the process that we needed to evaluate our own set of values. The Bible says, "Do not be conformed to this world, but be transformed by the renewing of your mind, that you may prove what is that good and acceptable and perfect will of God" (Rom. 12:2).

Values. We began to tackle the subject in the office of the King of the Cowboys over many cups of lukewarm coffee. Y' know what I mean?

Carole C. Carlson

Who Buried America's Values?

1

Stand fast therefore in the liberty by which Christ has made us free, and do not be entangled again with a yoke of bondage.

Galatians 5:1

SINCE WORLD WAR II, I have seen this nation slipping from its glory. During that time when we were all working for a common cause, there was a purpose in our unity. I remember going with the radio gang from *The Chase and Sanborn Hour* and entertaining the troops. In those days Edgar Bergen's dummy Charlie McCarthy may have been sassy, but he wasn't dirty. If we had ratings, our shows all would have been G.

Those years were an all-out effort to pre-serve freedom, and it cost the lives of hun-dreds of thousands of our young men. When the troops returned and stepped into civilian life, many of them couldn't find jobs because some women refused to step down from the wartime necessity to work, taking pay cuts to keep their jobs. I'm not against women work-ing; I've done it all my life. But in spite of the Ozzie and Harriet image of the 1950s, the place of more and more women working out-side the home had become established. Small cracks in the American family were beginning to appear.

When you have lived as long as I have, you have seen many changes. Technology and com-munication have accelerated like the rising of yeast rolls in a warm oven. I've written most of my books on a yellow lined tablet, scrawled with a pen in airports, lonely hotel rooms, or wherever the spirit moves me. Now my great-grandchildren (thirty of them at this count) have access to computers, CD-ROM, the Inter-net, and all types of complicated tools that the founders of this Republic would never have dreamed possible.

But have we improved morally and ethically in the same ratio as we have scientifically? Someone has said that man's maximum achievement often falls short of God's minimum demands.

I have witnessed the growing permissiveness in the schools. The front page of a Southern California newspaper recently carried the story of students who went on a hunger strike because they objected to a decision by the board of regents of that school system. The protesters worked a crowd into a jeering frenzy by shouting, "No justice! No peace!" and, "People united will never be divided." But those protests are mild stuff compared to what is happening in many of our schools.

How far have we gone when schools need fences to keep out criminals? When children are gunned down in drive-by shootings? Precious children. I get beside myself seeing such things!

How did the American Dream become so tarnished? Our forefathers came here to escape religious intolerance, but now we see that very intolerance flourishing. God has blessed America bountifully. Will we continue to enjoy that blessing at our present rate of decay?

The Columbus Controversy

In 1992 we experienced the Columbus quincentenary. My goodness, what a flurry that made! It turned out to be more of a controversy than a celebration. Every newsmagazine and the major Protestant and Catholic organizations hotly debated what Columbus's landing really meant. I wondered what all the fuss was about until I realized that the discovery of America was spearheaded by a man who believed God had a destiny for him. Peter Marshall and David Manuel wrote an outstanding book, *The Light and the Glory,* in which they quoted from an obscure volume of Columbus's that had never previously appeared in English. Here is just a short excerpt from that journal:

> It was the Lord who put into my mind (I could feel His hand upon me) the fact that it would be possible to sail from here to the Indies. All who heard of my project rejected it with laughter, ridi-

culing me. There is no question that the inspiration was from the Holy Spirit, because He comforted me with rays of marvelous inspiration from the Holy Scriptures.[1]

Isn't that amazing? I had never heard his faith emphasized. Yet to hear some folks shout "foul" during that five-hundred-year anniversary was enough to think that he was the most devious of men. The National Council of Churches was quoted as issuing this statement:

What some historians have termed a "discovery," in reality was an invasion and colonization with legalized occupation, genocide, economic exploitation, and a deep level of institutional racism and moral decadence.[2]

Excuse me . . . now Columbus is branded as a murderer and a racist? Are history books being rewritten?

Legacy of the Pilgrims and Puritans

Calling America a Christian nation today brings cries of protest. We are a country of great diversity, providing opportunity and freedom to people of every nationality and religion, but we must never forget that the values of those first immigrants were based on Christian principles.

I am told that 101 Pilgrims crammed into a space about the size of a volleyball court and spent sixty-six stormy, sickening, stinking days in the inner bowels of a little ship called the *Mayflower*. It's hard to imagine what it would be like confined in such a prison, but I've nursed enough sick children to know that even in the best of circumstances it can be challenging. These folks, however, had a dream to build a life in the New World where they could worship their God in freedom, away from the yoke of the Church of England. Hardships were part of the price.

What must it have been like for those brave folks—undernourished, sick, fearful of what they would encounter in this new land? And then to arrive in November on the East Coast! (I've been a California gal for so long that I get chills opening the refrigerator.)

They believed they were in the Promised Land, even though there were no houses, no roads, and no food. Not exactly a paradise on earth. Before anyone was allowed ashore, all the men signed the Mayflower Compact, promising to submit themselves to the laws enacted by

16

the whole group. Once ashore, William Bradford, a Pilgrim Father, led in a prayer of thanksgiving for delivering them from the perils of the sea and bringing them to America.

All they had to do then was contend with cold, starvation, sickness, and hostile Indians. No problem.

Those Pilgrims were a dedicated group. Living in the desert as I do, it's hard for me to imagine what it would be like in a New England winter, with the men trying to build shelter with hands that were almost frozen, and women trying to feed and warm their children. They soon developed scurvy or died of pneumonia.

In January the roof of the nearly completed common house caught fire, and much of their clothing was burned. By the time spring arrived, they had lost nearly half of their original number. One by one they were buried in the rocky soil.

I know the heartache of losing children. To go on with life is a wrenching experience.

The high point of the week was Sunday worship, when the "beat of a field drum would summon them to the morning and afternoon services."[3]

After that first rugged year, the Pilgrims were blessed with a bountiful harvest from their gardens, and furthermore, in October a crowd of friendly Indians arrived with wild turkeys and other game to celebrate and feast with their new friends. The first Thanksgiving was proclaimed by Governor William Bradford. Here's what Bradford wrote:

> As one small candle may light a thousand, so the light kindled here has shown unto many, yea in some sort to our whole nation. . . . We have noted these things so that you might see their worth and not negligently lose what your fathers have obtained with so much hardship.[4]

Today we use little Pilgrim decorations on our Thanksgiving tables and name banks and companies after the *Mayflower,* but we know little of the Pilgrim commitment.

The Puritans were a different breed from the Pilgrims, although both groups were Christians who believed in freedom. The Puritans believed they could live the life to which Christ had called them without separating themselves from the Church of England. They left bawdy, lawless England to establish a Christian community in a new land, thinking they could build the kingdom of God on earth. Those brave men and women made a covenant to live as Christ would have them live in this new land.

A covenant is a commitment to Christ and to one another that we seldom hear about today. It is a *binding* agreement. In rocky New England, God was raising up churches built on stone foundations (Matt. 7:24–27). The Puritans took sin seriously and, consequently, aroused the hatred of Satan. (Lest you wonder if I believe in the reality of Satan, let me emphasize that I do. If Jesus believed in him, then why should I deny his existence?) The Puritans, though, have had bad press in our time. They have been depicted as killjoys who were witchhunting bigots. To be called "puritanical" is an insult, conjuring up an image of a stiff-necked woman looking down her pince-nez at everyone and everything. The Puritans, for all of their self-righteousness and mistakes, deserve a heap of credit for the direction of our nation.

Backdrop for the Revolution

Before George Washington became the leading man in the great American epic, a few great ministers set New England ablaze with their preaching. Jonathan Edwards, who has been called one of America's greatest Christian thinkers, lit the flame that started what was called the Great Awakening. He preached his most famous sermon, "Sinners in the Hands of an Angry God," in 1741. Now that was a hellfire and brimstone message if there ever was one! (Most modern preachers water that down until it's more like toasted marshmallows.)

Real revival began to sweep through New England, and then along came George Whitefield. He was a fellow whose voice was legendary. His good friend, Benjamin Franklin, once calculated that (in a day before loudspeakers) Whitefield could have been heard by thirty thousand people! Incidentally, Franklin funded a building in Philadelphia for Whitefield to preach in, which later became the University of Pennsylvania.

According to the journal *Christian History,* Whitefield was the most popular figure in America before George Washington.

The first great revival in America where thousands of people accepted Jesus as their Savior brought tremendous spiritual renewal as well as advanced the cause of education. Dartmouth, Princeton, Rutgers, and Brown found their origins in Christian outreach.[5]

Although I cannot call myself an intellectual, I do not believe it is fair to label Christians as anti-intellectuals. Our American roots have been grown in the halls of ivy.

Our Buried History

Carole and I were shocked to read that more than half of America's high school seniors don't know basic facts about U.S. history. In the scores that were released in the month we began this book, November 1995, here were the results: "The history test, given to a national sample of 22,500 fourth, eighth, and twelfth graders found among twelfth graders, only 43 percent attained at least the basic level; 11 percent were proficient; and 1 percent advanced."[6]

Parents, educators, school boards, this is our call for action. It is time to teach the truth of our American roots and instill a pride in our heritage.

Value of Our American Heritage

2

It cannot be emphasized too strongly or too often that this great nation was founded, not by religionists, but by Christians; not on religions, but on the Gospel of Jesus Christ. For this very reason peoples of other faiths have been afforded asylum, prosperity, and freedom of worship here.

Patrick Henry, 1765

"AMERICA WAS NOT founded as a Christian nation" is a statement I find hard to swallow. The "Christian Conservative Right" is accused of twisting history to suit its views. On the contrary, I believe the facts contradict that accusation.

Who were the influential men who established our Constitution? What were the basic beliefs of those men and women who founded our great universities, formed our government, and led our nation to greatness? Were they atheists? Buddhists? Muslims? Agnostics?

Our American heritage is under attack by a worldview that is the opposite of that of our Founding Fathers.

Excuse me if I do some flag-waving now. The reputations of some of my heroes are at stake.

George Washington, a Christian

Cherry pies may make us think of George Washington, but the father of our country was a man with deep Christian convictions. Washington's mother was a strong influence on his spiritual life. When he was about twenty, he wrote in a little book some prayers that set the tone for his life. The manuscript was found in the stacks of the Yale Divinity School Library.

We can almost hear him speak in these beautiful prayers.

Sunday Morning: Let my heart, therefore, gracious God, be so affected with the glory and majesty of Thine honor that I may not do mine own works,

but wait on Thee, and discharge those weighty
duties which Thou requirest of me . . .

Monday Morning: Direct my thoughts, words and
work, wash away my sins in the immaculate Blood
of the Lamb, and purge my heart by Thy Holy
Spirit . . . daily frame me more and more in the
likeness of Thy Son Jesus Christ.[1]

The legend of the cherry tree and "I cannot
tell a lie" may be the only thing a schoolchild
will remember about Washington, but his
legacy to America is the reminder that our first
president was a devout Christian.

History books today may tell of the winter
of 1777 when Gen. George Washington and
his troops were camped at Valley Forge, where
soldiers died at the rate of twelve a day and suffered the freezing cold without blankets or even
shoes. The feet and legs of many soldiers turned
black with frostbite and had to be amputated.
The miracle of Valley Forge is that the men
endured at all. The prayers and beliefs of their
general sustained them when they could have
lost hope. But do the history books tell of
Washington's prayers or strong faith?

A pastor of a church near Valley Forge, one of the founders of the Lutheran Church in America, said this about Washington:

> I heard a fine example today, namely that His Excellency General Washington rode around among his army yesterday and admonished each and every one to fear God, to put away the wickedness that has set in, and to practice the Christian virtues. From all appearances, this gentleman does not belong to the so-called world of society, for he respects God's Word, believes in the atonement through Christ, and bears himself in humility and gentleness. Therefore, the Lord God has also singularly, yea marvelously preserved him from harm in the midst of countless perils, ambuscades, fatigues, etc., and has hitherto graciously held him in His hand as a chosen vessel.[2]

When the Revolutionary War was over, the thirteen states were far from being united. In 1787 delegates gathered in Philadelphia for the Constitutional Convention. The quarrels among the states were worse than a large family trying to decide where to have a reunion. The "perfect union" was a perfect mess.

God placed Washington as president of that stormy convention that was to set the course for our country. Historian Page Smith wrote:

His genius was the ability to endure, to maintain his equilibrium in the midst of endless frustrations, disappointments, setbacks and defeats. . . . George Washington became the symbol of the American colonists' determination to endure.[3]

Where do we think Washington got his endurance? Washington himself gives credit to God and prayer. When he was unanimously elected as president of the Constitutional Convention, he said, "Let us raise a standard to which the wise and the honest can repair; the event is in the Hand of God."[4]

The states were arguing over their "sovereign rights" like children over the biggest cookie. Just when it looked as if the debate over representation had deadlocked the entire proceedings, God used an elder statesman, a man who was not an outspoken Christian, to further his plans for our country. Benjamin Franklin, eighty-one-year-old scientist and inventor, said:

In the beginning of the contest with Britain, when we were sensible of danger, we had daily prayers in this room for Divine protection. Our prayers, Sir, were heard, and they were graciously answered. All of us who were engaged in the struggle must have observed frequent instances of a superintending Providence in our favor. . . . And have we now forgotten this powerful Friend? Or do we imagine we no longer need His assistance?

I have lived, Sir, a long time, and the longer I live, the more convincing proofs I see of this truth: "that God governs in the affairs of man." And if a sparrow cannot fall to the ground without His notice, is it probable that an empire can rise without His aid?

We have been assured, Sir, in the Sacred Writings that except the Lord build the house, they labor in vain that build it. I firmly believe this.[5]

The majority of those men who formed the Constitution and the Bill of Rights were Christians. There is no doubt about the beliefs of our first president. Thanks to God, the new nation was getting off to a good start.

Was Lincoln a Christian?

Some people disagree over the beliefs of Abraham Lincoln. Although his profession of faith was not as open as Washington's, his actions point toward a Christian commitment. We came across a copy of a remarkable little book called *Lincoln's Devotional,* which was published in 1852 and inscribed by Lincoln.

Agnostics do not usually keep a book of prayer in their possession.

Judge for yourself. Here are a few statements he made:

> I have been driven many times upon my knees by the overwhelming conviction that I had nowhere else to go. My own wisdom, and that of all about me, seemed insufficient for that day. . . .
>
> In the very responsible position in which I happen to be placed, being a humble instrument in the hands of our Heavenly Father, as I am, and as we all are, to work out His great purposes, I have desired that all my works and acts may be according to His will, and that it might be so, I have sought His aid.

His own pastor at the New York Avenue Presbyterian Church said that "the death of Willie Lincoln (his twelve-year-old son) in 1862 and the visit to the Gettysburg battlefield in 1863 finally led Lincoln to personal faith in Christ."[6]

Why debate this issue anymore?

Beliefs of Other American Leaders

In his inaugural address on March 4, 1925, Calvin Coolidge said: "America seeks no empires built on blood and forces . . . she cherishes no purpose save to merit the favor of Almighty God."

Theodore Roosevelt, the twenty-sixth president of the United States, soldier, author, and Nobel Peace Prize winner, said, "A thorough knowledge of the Bible is worth more than a college education." (I appreciate that statement, since I never went to college.)

In one of his famous fireside chats, President Franklin D. Roosevelt said: "We cannot read the history of our rise and development as a nation, without reckoning with the place the Bible has occupied in shaping the advances of the Republic."

During the darkest days of World War II, and I remember them well, Roosevelt met with British Prime Minister Winston Churchill on a ship in the mid-Atlantic. Roosevelt asked the crew of that American ship to join him in a chorus of "Onward, Christian Soldiers" and described the United States as "the lasting concord between men and nations, *founded on the principles of Christianity*" (emphasis mine!).

Did you know that the "under God" part of the pledge of allegiance was added in 1954 during the Eisenhower administration?

Forty years later, some in America want it eliminated.

A Christian Manifesto

One of our great Christian intellectuals was Francis Schaeffer. When he spoke at the Coral Ridge Presbyterian Church in Florida, he put America's value system in perspective. It wasn't a pleasant picture.

Schaeffer said that Christians are just plain stupid about the lessons of history. "Where have the Bible-believing Christians been in the past forty years?" he asked.

He pointed out that the predominant world-view is humanistic, which places man as the measure of all things. Man must generate values himself, without knowledge from God. This, he said, is the opposite of what the Founding Fathers believed.

Schaeffer warned that when we cut ourselves loose from the law of God, we have a relativistic value system. "We must recognize that this country is almost lost," Schaeffer stated.

As Dale and I (Carole) watched the video of that speech, we wanted to disagree with Francis Schaeffer. America is not lost; it is just wandering. Her people are beginning to wake up and learn the truth about values and ethics again.

We had been involved in some pretty deep thoughts when Dale leaned back in Roy's brown leather chair and asked, "What is truth? Is it really all relative?" She gave me her penetrating look that seemed to expect some definitive answer.

I said, "Let's have lunch."

Is Truth Dead?

3

> I have chosen the way of truth; I have set
> my heart on your laws.
>
> Psalm 119:30 NIV

A LIE IS LIKE a twisted ball of yarn. When
you try to find the end, you only get more
entangled. Early in my acting career, I became
involved in a deception that I rationalized
because of personal ambition. My career was
more important than my honesty.

It all began when I was a rebellious high
school kid and eloped with a handsome boy,
both of us lying about our ages to get a marriage license. The marriage was a terrible failure, but I was blessed with a wonderful son,

Tom. My faithful mother helped me raise him, or I would have been destitute.

As Tom began to grow, I was determined to provide an education and a good life for him. I took him to church, believing that he needed to know the Lord and live by his principles. As for me, I had begun to sing with dance bands, on radio, and in fancy hotels. I believed that Jesus might make demands on me that would interfere with my career, so I avoided making a commitment to him. My integrity was blinded by ambition.

The test really came when I was summoned to Hollywood for a screen test. My son was twelve years old and I was twenty-eight. Being that age and having a son that old were unacceptable for a leading lady in the movie industry of the 1940s. The solution was for me to say that I was twenty-one and that Tom was my brother. I agreed to that bald-faced lie in order to get a contract with Twentieth Century-Fox.

As my career progressed, my guilt grew. Tom became a dedicated young Christian, and one day he told me he couldn't lie as I was lying, even for me. That hurt. But I was too far into the mud to be able to climb out.

Years later, God convicted me of my deceit. That story is told in the next chapter. However, I can understand how the desires of the heart, if not guided by God's principles, can squeeze you into the world's mold. Lying can become such a habit that even the liar does not know what the truth is.

Truth: Endangered Species

Several years ago, Allan Bloom, a professor at the University of Chicago, made some startling observations. He shook the academic community with his statements about modern education. He said:

> There is one thing a professor can be absolutely certain of: almost every student entering the university believes, or says he believes, that truth is relative. . . . Relativism is necessary to openness; and this is the virtue, the only virtue, which all primary education for more than fifty years has dedicated itself to inculcating. Openness—and the relativism that makes it the only plausible stance in the face of various claims to truth and various ways of life and kinds of human beings— is the great insight of our times. The true believer is the real danger. . . . The point is not to correct

the mistakes and really be right; rather it is not to think you are right at all.[1]

If Bloom was correct, and I believe he was, then our educational system is spawning young men and women who have no conception of right and wrong. If truth is relative, then what or who are they to believe? Their parents? The most popular professor? Current political thought?

Someone said that labels should be on jars of jam, not people, but today we label people for identification. "Baby Busters" is a label applied to those people born between 1965 and 1983. George Barna, who heads a research group that makes statistics interesting, said in his book *Baby Busters: The Disillusioned Generation,* that "to the typical Buster, there is no such thing as absolute truth. Statistically, 70% claim that all truth is relative and personal."[2]

These kids are saying that nothing can be known for certain except the things they experience in their own lives. They have been told, "Do what comes naturally. If it feels good . . . do it."

Is it any wonder that we are facing a moral crisis in America? A free society cannot survive with people who habitually lie, cheat, and have no standards of truth. When children want to accuse someone of fibbing, they point their fingers and chant, "Liar, liar, pants on fire." We should be burning with shame for becoming people who cannot be trusted.

I can remember when a man's handshake was his word. Today we sign contracts in triplicate.

Time magazine had a story a few years ago with one of the ugliest pictures on the cover that I've ever seen. It was a close-up of a grinning face leering at you with a diabolical smile. The title was, "Lying . . . everybody's doin' it (honest)." The article was an indictment against politicians. "The public may now assume lying on the part of its representatives because it expects them to lie."[3]

For government to be effective, we need some degree of honesty. I don't look at what our representatives say; I examine who they are. What are their bedrock beliefs? Do they just mouth a belief in God, or do they live it?

The Busters are not the only disillusioned ones. In a magazine for senior citizens (about forty million of us), it was said, "America is headed straight to hell, figuratively and literally, unless it changes course soon."[4]

Listen to the statistics from the senior category (who should know better!). Answering the question, "What's the best way to halt declining values?" the largest number, 35 percent, answered, "Shore up governmental and personal responsibility." Yet how can moral decline be halted if neither government nor individuals have a standard for truth?

The Book of Truth

One of our most popular presidents was Dwight Eisenhower, who was commander of Allied forces in Europe during World War II and president of the United States from 1953 to 1961.

Roy and I, along with the Riders of the Purple Sage, were invited to Washington to entertain for David Eisenhower's birthday. I'll never forget a conversation I had with Mamie Eisenhower. She said, "We still sleep in the same bed, and sometimes at night I wake up and find him gone. He's usually in the garden, pacing back and forth and praying for guidance."

I guess I knew that Ike was a Christian but I never realized the depth of his belief. He was a president who built his life on the words of the Bible to a greater degree than most people know. He said,

> The Bible is endorsed by the ages. Our civilization is built upon its words. Like stored wisdom, the lessons of the Bible are useless unless they are lifted out and employed. A faithful reading of Scripture provides the courage and strength required for the living of our time.[5]

It doesn't do any good to have millions of Bibles on bookshelves unless the truths within their pages are applied to our lives. It doesn't do any good for a witness to place his hand on the Bible and swear to tell "the whole truth, nothing but the truth, so help me God" unless the Bible is the basis of that person's belief system. He might as well swear on a comic book!

Jesus said, "I am the way, the truth, and the life. No one comes to the Father except through me" (John 14:6). When you think of it, probably no other words ever said have been more disputed than those. There is only one way to

God and that is through faith in Jesus Christ. And that is the truth.

Verily, Verily

In the King James Version of the Bible, we read over and over that Jesus said, "Verily, verily," which in the newer translations is "I tell you the truth . . . I tell you the truth." If Jesus did not tell us the truth, millions of people throughout history have been living the big lie. If Jesus did not tell us the truth, my life has been based on a fraud.

Jesus had been arrested in the Garden of Gethsemane, bound, beaten, and dragged to Pilate's court. Imagine the scene. Jesus, charged with rebellion, stood before the Roman governor of Judea and was asked, "Are you the king of the Jews?" (John 18:33 NIV).

Jesus did not look like a king; he did not live like a king; so the men who guarded him jeered and mocked. Jesus answered: "You are right in saying I am a king. In fact, for this reason I was born, and for this I came into the world, to testify to the truth. Everyone on the side of truth listens to me" (John 18:37 NIV).

Pilate answered with that universal question, "What is truth?" (John 18:38 NIV).

Why didn't Pilate understand that Jesus had just told him that he was truth? Sometimes when faced with such clear and simple statements, a person can't understand. When I hear some of the complicated gobbledygook that people use to rationalize the truth of God, I think if they had actually been present at the trial of the ages, they would have sided with Pilate.

Jesus has told us over and over again in the Bible that he was telling us the truth. Here are just a few examples:

> I tell you the truth, anyone who will not receive the kingdom of God like a little child will never enter it. (Luke 18:17 NIV)
> In reply Jesus declared, "I tell you the truth, no one can see the kingdom of God unless he is born again." (John 3:3 NIV)
> I tell you the truth, he who believes has everlasting life. (John 6:47 NIV)

The Bible also warns us that not everyone will rush to put out a welcome mat for the truth:

41

Even from your own number men will arise and distort the truth in order to draw away disciples after them. (Acts 20:30 NIV)

Many will follow their shameful ways and will bring the way of truth into disrepute. (2 Peter 2:2 NIV)

They exchanged the truth of God for a lie, and worshiped and served created things rather than the Creator—who is forever praised. Amen. (Rom. 1:25)

Many are trying to kill truth today, but the Bible says that if we take the sword of the Spirit, which is the Word of God, we can extinguish all the flaming arrows of the evil one (see Eph. 6:13–18).

Truth is not dead. It can be found in the Bible I hold in my hand right now. Truth is alive for now and eternity.

My Search for Life's Values

4

> I love the LORD, because He has heard my voice.
>
> Psalm 116:1

MY STORY HAS BEEN TOLD in more detail in *The Woman at the Well,* but a capsule version of it is needed here to give the background on how my life was one continual search for solid values.

I was born Frances Octavia Smith and was a real handful growing up. I didn't live up to the dignity of my name. As the spoiled first grandchild, I wanted to be the center of attention and did my best to stay there.

One of my earliest memories is going to a little Baptist church in Italy, Texas, where my

mother played the piano. I loved music and sometimes when a hand-clapping gospel song began, I would scoot out of our pew and dance in the aisle. That just wasn't done in a Baptist church.

A switch was frequently applied to my backside; but my psyche was never injured, just my pride. I shudder to think of what I might have been if no one cared enough to discipline me.

Granddaddy Wood was a great influence in my life. He never lost his zest for living or his love for children. When I was very small, he said something about me that was almost prophetic. "She'll die hard, with her head up!" Many times I've recalled those words of Grandpa's. When life has dealt me tough blows, I've been given the strength to handle them and come back bruised but not broken.

I was blessed with a Christian upbringing, although I shoved it in the background in later years. This should give hope to parents of prodigal sons or daughters. Teach the little ones now; grasp the few years of their childhood and point them toward Jesus. Solomon said, "Remember now your Creator in the days of your youth, before the difficult days come" (Eccles. 12:1).

Both my father and mother went to Christian colleges and instilled in me the importance of education. They taught me how to read and do simple arithmetic before I entered school, so I skipped half of the first grade, all of the second, and went right into the third grade. I don't believe that was wise, because children miss too many valuable experiences when they are forced to grow up fast. But I loved school and I also loved music. I started taking piano lessons but I soon became impatient with those endless exercises and began to improvise. My poor piano teacher told my parents that I was wasting her time and their money. She gave up on me. I played by ear from then on and music has been a part of my life and career. It must have been a part of God's plan that I never turned into a whiz at the piano.

Sundays we went to Sunday school, church, and an evangelistic service at 7:30 in the evening. I was expected to be there, and it never dawned on me to goof off and not go until I reached my early teens. When parents ask me today, "Should I make my children go to church?" I usually ask them if they go to church. If they say yes, then I'm free to say, "Don't you think your children should go where you're going?" If they say no, I ask, "Then why should you expect your children to go?"

I don't want to give the impression that church-going makes a person a Christian. I remember Corrie ten Boom saying, "A mouse in a cookie jar isn't a cookie!" On the other hand, I do believe that Christians who think they can worship without church attendance are only fooling themselves. The Bible says, "Let us not neglect our church meetings, as some people do, but encourage and warn each other, especially now that the day of his coming back again is drawing near" (Heb. 10:25 LB).

When I was a kid, church and school were partners in training children. In school we began each day with a short prayer and had chapel every Friday morning, with different ministers giving a devotional. Even those kids who didn't go to church got a dose of Bible teaching. I don't know of anyone suing the school board for allowing such outrageous teaching! I believe it is a tragic mistake that separation of church and state has been so misinterpreted that God is left out of the classroom.

When I was ten, our church had an old-time revival meeting with an itinerant evangelist. He talked a lot about hell, and I decided it wasn't a place I wanted to go. I walked down the aisle and received Jesus Christ as my Savior. However, for many years I refused to surrender my life wholeheartedly to him.

I wanted to run things my way, thank you.

My mother used to say I was "born grown." It was that attitude that caused the first serious problem in my life.

Too Young to Marry

When kids go astray, parents often blame themselves. "What did we do wrong?" they moan. My parents may have made mistakes, but it wasn't their fault that I became rebellious. I was only fourteen when I started going with a handsome boy who was a few years older than me. When our relationship looked like it was getting out of hand, I was forbidden to see him. Defying my parents' wishes, I met him secretly. One day we decided to elope. Lying about our ages, we obtained a marriage license and were wed in the home of a minister.

I shall never forget the agonizing silence on the other end of the phone when I called my mother to tell her we were married. When she finally spoke, it was to ask us to come home. We went home the next day.

Mother pleaded with me to go back to high school since I had another year before graduation. Still in defiance of authority, I refused.

Tom was born, and when he was six months old, his father announced that he was too young to be tied down. I was only sixteen and already facing divorce.

The Critical Decade

Dr. James Dobson calls the years between sixteen and twenty-six "the critical decade." I think every decade is critical, but that period was a time of searching for my purpose in life. Trying to deal with the pain of a ruined marriage and support a child, I struggled to find my way.

Church became important to me again, and I began to read my Bible. I was told I needed to learn a skill; so I went to business school, although my heart was in show business. While working as a secretary, I even tried writing short stories. After the rejection slips piled up, I was convinced I would never get anything published.

After work I spent most of my time singing and accompanying myself on the piano. One day the big chance came to be a guest on a radio program. It was the foot in the door I needed. From radio, I began to get opportunities to sing with dance bands. Then I decided that if I could crack the market in small towns, I could win in the Windy City. So I took Tommy and went to Chicago. A few struggling years later, however, I lost the fight. Sick and broke, I wired my folks for money and went home to Texas.

My precious mother cared for Tommy while I regained my strength. He called her Mom and me Sassie. (Frances was too hard to pronounce.) She was more of a mother to him in those early years than I was. I was more like a big sister.

My ambition drove me and dominated my life. One time Tommy was very sick during a polio epidemic. I was frantic with fear as he was taken to the hospital for a spinal tap. I promised God that I would put him first in my life if my son's test was negative. It was.

For a few weeks I prayed and read my Bible every day. But once again, my relationship with God took a backseat to my musical ambition.

Overnight success is the stuff movies and fairy tales are made of. One value I learned early on was to work hard. I was on the staff of a Louisville, Kentucky, station when I met a pianist-arranger who became my husband. It looked like that rainbow was within reach. We went to Chicago, and this time I began to sing at the fancy hotel ballrooms. Frances Smith was transformed into Dale Evans. Show business became my life.

Sure, I took Tom to church because I wanted him to have a solid relationship with the Lord; but as for me, I held back from an all-out commitment, afraid that the Lord might demand something from me that I was not willing to give. He might even ask me to give up my career, and I wasn't willing to do that.

Hollywood, though, was not my goal. I wanted to do musical comedy in New York. Besides, I didn't think I was pretty enough for the movies, and I certainly did not consider myself an actress. One day, however, I got a telegram from an agent in California. This was heady stuff. Without going into all the steps that led me to the glitter capital of the world, let me just say that this was a time when my values were not as important as the tinsel in the studios. This was when I lied about my age and tried to pass off Tom as my brother.

Something was very wrong with my life. No amount of busyness filled the emptiness I felt. I went to church with Tom and my husband, but between Sundays I read books on peace of mind, Eastern philosophy, and even mysticism.

World War II was in full swing, and I did a lot of shows for the boys in the service. Because we were so busy, my husband and I were seeing less and less of each other. I was making four hundred dollars a week and working like a Texas ranch hand. While America was unified in the war effort, my husband and I were drifting further apart.

With my "critical decade" closing, I lived with a sense of failure and an emptiness of spirit.

Riding the Career Bronco

By the time I met Roy Rogers, I had encountered enough Hollywood types to know the difference between the real thing and a phony. Roy was genuine. When I landed a contract to play opposite him in a film, I neglected to tell anyone that I couldn't ride a horse. The first day on location I was put to the test. There was a horse that looked as big as a barn to me, and I didn't even know which side to get on. Roy just looked at me with that crinkly-eyed smile of his and said, "I thought you could ride."

Believe me, after several near disasters, I did learn to ride.

Roy was a straight-shooter in every way. In the studio, we were a family: Roy, Gabby Hayes, Pat Brady, the Sons of the Pioneers, and me. We made more than thirty films and knew the best and the worst of each other. The worst of me was my growing ego.

The drive for personal success is a factor that unbalances any life. My ambition was like a runaway stallion. I didn't realize it then but I was sacrificing the most precious things in life to satisfy my personal desires.

In 1945 my husband and I were divorced. I was more devoted to the demands of the Hollywood system than to our marriage. We had working hours that kept us apart. I was a day person, and he was a musician and a night person.

Meanwhile, "back at the ranch," my son Tom was being nurtured through those crucial teen years by my mother. He had developed into a fine Christian, no thanks to me. Oh sure, I had declared my faith in God and in Jesus Christ, but it was on the back burner, and the fire wasn't on.

God's Mysterious Ways

Roy was married to Arline, a very pretty girl, and they had two children: Cheryl, an adopted daughter who was a Shirley Temple look-alike, and Linda Lou, a quiet child with sparkling eyes. Roy was proud of his girls. Church and Sunday school, though, were not a part of their life. Roy had told us during gab sessions on the set that he could not reconcile a loving God with the suffering he saw when he visited children's hospitals all over the country. He had questions I could not answer.

Arline gave birth to Roy Jr., by cesarean section, but she died eight days later because of a blood clot following surgery. Roy was devastated.

After Arline's death, Roy struggled to find help to run his home and care for his children. He worked unbelievably long hours and made personal appearance tours to make the money he needed to support his family.

As time went on, we realized that our relationship was deepening beyond our movie partnership. However, neither of us wanted to rush into marriage.

I must say, I probably had one of the most unromantic proposals in the book. We were sitting on our horses in the chutes during a rodeo in the Chicago Stadium. It was in the fall of 1947. Roy leaned over his saddle and said, "What are you doing New Year's Eve?" That seemed rather strange to me, since New Year's Eve was months away.

We were waiting to be introduced and have the gates opened for us to gallop out before the crowd. I said, "No plans."

He said, "Well, why don't we get married?"

I said, "Yes!" and just then the announcer shouted, "And now, the King of the Cowboys and the Queen of the West . . . Roy Rogers and Dale Evans!"

In 1947 I understood very little of God's mysterious ways.

House Built on Rock

When we were married on New Year's Eve, we thought we were keeping it a secret. The intrepid Louella Parsons, though, who seemed to know everything about everybody in Tinseltown, broke the news on radio and also broadcast that I had a grown son. Frankly, Tom and I were relieved that the long deception I had played was over.

As Roy and I began to build our life together, we faced many challenges. First of all, I was a stepmother. I hadn't considered myself a very good mother to my own Tom, but now there were three more. My career had to take a backseat with the new responsibilities. It was all so overwhelming.

Tom was a teenager but with wisdom beyond his years. He suggested that God could help me do what I felt inadequate to do. And he thought I should take the children to church. The next Sunday I went to an evening service with him.

The preacher gave a sermon on "The House That Is Built on the Rock." He said that any house built on the rock of faith in Jesus Christ would stand up against anything that life could throw at you. I thought about my ego, my lies, all my failures, and it seemed like my very soul was shouting, "You are guilty, Dale Evans Rogers. You are a sinner."

Until that time, I thought a sinner was the drunk who staggered down Main Street or the producer who demanded the starlet to sleep with him. Then I realized that Scripture says, "*All* have sinned and fall short of the glory of God" (Rom. 3:23, emphasis added).

Even though I had walked the aisle many years before, the following Sunday I bounced out of my pew and rushed forward. This time when I gave my life to Christ, it was more than lip service. I asked him to forgive me and accept me just as I was. *This time* I asked him to create in me a right spirit, to break me if he had to. I surrendered my life to use for his glory.

How can I describe the peace that came over me? The emptiness in my life was gone; in its place was a joy that surpassed anything I had ever experienced. Now when I sang "How Great Thou Art," I knew the meaning of the words.

Roy was less than thrilled when I burst into the house and said, "Honey, I've just made the greatest decision of my life; I've dedicated my heart and life to Jesus Christ!"

Roy was glad to see me so enthusiastic but he must have chosen his words carefully, for he said, "Mama, if it makes you happy, fine. But please don't go overboard and don't go to work on me."

He said those words in a spirit of love, and I accepted them that way. I loved him too much to force him into his own decision.

I began taking the children to Sunday school and church, reading the Bible at dinner, and hearing their prayers. Roy started to notice a change in me, although he didn't say anything. One Sunday, after a rip-roarin' Saturday night argument following a party at our house, Roy announced that he was going to church with us. When the sermon was over, as was the custom in that church, an invitation to accept Christ was given. Roy sat straight up (he had his eyes closed during the sermon, and I thought he was dozing) and said, "Mama, I'm going down there."

Roy made his own decision, without any prodding from me, and I was never happier in my life. Now our house was truly being built on a Rock. Gradually God began to break this ego and pride of mine and show me his values for my life.

5   Value of Tough Times

> We are hard pressed on every side, yet not crushed; we are perplexed, but not in despair; persecuted, but not forsaken; struck down, but not destroyed.
>
> 2 Corinthians 4:8–9

THE BIBLE HAS RED LIGHTS. Sometimes I've breezed through the warning signs without stopping. One that slowed me down, however, was raised by an old fisherman named Peter. He said, "Do not think it strange concerning the fiery trial which is to try you, as though some strange thing happened to you" (1 Peter 4:12).

The best way to survive those fiery trials is by holding the hand of the Lord. When the three Hebrew youths were thrown into the furnace by order of Nebuchadnezzar, they walked out unscathed. Walking with them was their fourth companion—Jesus. Without him, they would have been a heap of charred bones.

Are we Christians prepared to be persecuted for our faith? Have we prepared ourselves for tough times?

The Bible says, "All who desire to live godly in Christ Jesus will suffer persecution" (2 Tim. 3:12). And Jesus warned that as the time of his return comes closer, "They will lay their hands on you and persecute you" (Luke 21:12).

Now I'm not saying we should all get persecution complexes when tough times hit. Compared to Christians in many parts of the world, we Christians in America have had it pretty easy. However, in subtle ways we're beginning to see the foreshadowing of persecution happening now.

It's one thing to be labeled with derision as the "Christian Right," but it's another to be tortured for our faith.

Billy Graham asked the probing question:

Are we too soft, too used to the luxuries of freedom, that we would be unable to stand up to persecution? Most of us would do no more, no less, than we are doing right now. Some of us who wear our Christianity on our sleeves would probably be the first to surrender. Many would be modern-day Peters who would say, "Though all others deny Christ, yet I will never deny him." But he did. Three times.[1]

When you go into a jewelry store to look for a particular ring or necklace, the master jeweler will place a black velvet cloth on the counter so that the stone or chain will look its best. It has been said that we are God's jewels, and often he exhibits his gems on a dark background so they will shine more brightly too.

Some of us, though, need more polishing than others to show our value.

Tough times are as inevitable in life as ants at a picnic. None of us wants them; all of us will have them. Tough times come in many forms . . . the death of a loved one, sickness, financial woes, broken relationships. The good news is that we can be prepared, because God gives us the tools in his book to equip us.

Why Me?

The "Why me?" complex is common among the afflicted. I guess the correct answer would be, "Why not?" If life was all "Happy Trails," then we'd never know how to ride through the bristles and swamplands and deserts.

Lieutenant Clebe McClary lost one arm and an eye in a fierce grenade attack in Vietnam. This young man, a handsome, disciplined athlete, came home from the war with a shattered body and what he thought was a shattered life. Clebe wrote in his book, *Living Proof,* "I don't think my suffering was in vain. The Lord has used my experiences for good by drawing many lives to Him. It's hard to see any good that came from the war in Vietnam, but I don't believe our effort was wasted. Surely some seed was planted for Christ that cannot be stamped out."[2]

Barbara Johnson is a person who has taken life's blows and turned them into humor. In a world of so much tragedy, she is able to lighten the load with her own sense of compassionate joy. One chapter title in her book *Splashes of Joy in the Cesspools of Life* was "Laugh and the World Laughs with You . . . Cry and You Simply Get Wet."

From the tragedies in her life, Barbara has touched the lives of many who have forgotten how to laugh. Her ministry could be based on

Solomon's words: "To everything there is a season . . . a time to weep, and a time to laugh" (Eccles. 3:1, 4).

Life gives us bumps, but laughter is a shock absorber that eases the blows.

Many know the story of Joni Eareckson Tada, the beautiful woman who is a quadriplegic, permanently confined to a wheelchair. Joni paints by holding a brush with her teeth, writes with brilliance, and sings with joy in her heart. I have appeared on programs with her, and her testimony about the value of tough times touches us all.

Tim Hansel was an experienced mountain climber, but in one terrifying fall down a glacier, he was doomed to a lifetime of constant pain. He wrote in his book *You Gotta Keep Dancin'*, "I can't remember when I last woke up feeling good. Each morning continues another layer of nauseating pain, stiffness, the dull gray ache, and the never-ending fatigue. It's been a little over ten years since my accident. Life was different before then; I just can't remember what it felt like."[3]

Yet Hansel learned how to have joy in the midst of pain. One line in his diary said, "He who laughs . . . lasts."

Roy and I have tried to be ambassadors of joy to children around the world, but God used some of our own children to teach us the value of tears and tough times.

His Angels' Charge over Me

When God chose to give us little Robin Elizabeth, after doctors had told me I could not have another child, I knew before I left the hospital that there was something severely wrong with our little miracle baby. They told me she was mongoloid, and perhaps it would be better if we institutionalized her from the beginning.

Robin had been dedicated to the Lord, and in spite of our heartbreak, I felt that she would be used to glorify him in some way.

God took Robin home to be with him when she was two years old. Her story in the little book *Angel Unaware* went around the world. For the two years she was with us, she taught me some lasting lessons on true values in life.

What could a child with a severe disability teach us? She taught us that the strength of the Lord is made perfect through weakness. She taught us humility, patience, gratitude, and dependence on God.

As I look back more than forty-four years to the short time we had with Robin, I remember it was a period filled with heavy sadness and joyous excitement. After she died, I was driven (I think that's more accurate than "inspired") to write *Angel Unaware*.

People have asked me about the title of the book. It comes from Hebrews 13:1 (KJV): "Be not forgetful to entertain strangers; for thereby some have entertained angels unawares."

Only God himself could have taken that little book and turned it into a best-seller. Hundreds of thousands of people with exceptional children were able to find new confidence because God had spoken to them through Robin and through us.

Two months after Robin's death, we adopted a bright little Choctaw Indian baby we named Dodie; and shortly afterwards, Sandy, a five-year-old boy with physical and psychological problems, became a part of the family. In 1954 we took a foster child, Marion Fleming, from a church orphanage in Edinburgh, Scotland.

I believe Roy's heart was big enough to hold all the children of the world, and I just rode alongside him.

The Growing Years

When Dodie was three and a half, God brought us another blessing in the arms of Dr. Bob Pierce, the founder of World Vision. Little In Lee was a Korean orphan whom we named Debbie Lee, a child full of bubbling joy. Now we had Cheryl and Linda Lou, Dusty (Roy Jr.), Dodie, Sandy, Marion, and Debbie. Our hands were now full with seven young children, one grown son, two careers, and a challenge a minute.

We raised our blended family with discipline combined with unconditional love. But we had definite rules of behavior for the Rogers' clan.

Dusty and Sandy were a handful. They could be twin terrors. When I took them shopping, they sat in the backseat of the car. I carried a switch to referee their wrestling matches. Once I applied a swift sting of discipline to Dusty's derriere.

"Mom, I'm leaving home!" he howled. "Good idea," I said. "We'll pack your suitcase as soon as we get home." It was very quiet for a few minutes. "Well, maybe I'll wait a year or two," he mumbled under his breath.

Naughty or nice, I think children are terrific. Jesus certainly set the example for us when he told his disciples to bring the children to him. I have sung, "Jesus loves the little children, all the children of the world. Red and yellow, black and white, they are precious in His sight," so many times that when I see an adult neglecting, abusing, or spoiling a precious child, I am filled with revulsion and cannot find the words to describe my anger.

As the children grew, so did our faith. We became a part of the Hollywood Christian group, people who were prominent in the industry and bold enough to stand for Christ in a largely anti-Christian atmosphere. We had a meeting every Monday night in different homes. Billy Graham came to one of the first meetings in our backyard around the swimming pool. It was the beginning of a relationship that has spanned the years.

Roy says, "Every time Billy walks into a room the lights come on." We can testify to the fact that we are among the millions whose lives have been touched by this great man.

In the summer of 1963, Billy came to the Los Angeles Memorial Coliseum for a major crusade. This was a milestone for the Rogers family, for on Youth Night, Dusty, Sandy, Dodie, and Debbie went down the aisle onto that immense field and gave their hearts to Jesus. My cup was running over.

At the same crusade in 1963, my coauthor, Carole, said that her entire family accepted the Lord.

All of this is just a brief background to more of those tough times. How quickly our joy turned to sorrow. A year after Debbie dedicated her life to Christ, she met him face-to-face. In 1964 our precious twelve-year-old was killed in a church bus accident. I didn't think I could stand losing another child.

Roy was in the hospital after an operation, and his surgeon told him the wrenching news of Debbie's death. Because of Roy's hospitalization, we could not lean on each other's strength at this time. I don't know how people get through times like this without the Lord.

Soon after her funeral, I was guided (yes, that can happen) to write the book *Dearest Debbie* to help those mothers and fathers who might lose their Debbies.

And Then There Was Sandy

In 1965 our Sandy enlisted in the army. He had been a battered child and had physical and psychological injuries that never completely healed; but he wanted to prove himself worthy as a man, and the one way he knew how was to join the army. When we saw him off for basic training, I had a premonition that we might never see him again.

Sandy did come home once more, to become officially engaged. Then he was sent to Germany and, through a tragic accident, died in an army camp there. Some of his buddies dared him to chugalug to prove that he was man enough to wear his first-class stripes. He was killed by an overdose of alcohol during that "I dare you" drinking session.

In one of his letters to us, Sandy had written, "Put your faith in the Lord because He's always around when you need Him. All He asks in return is your heart and devotion."

No Pity Party

Roy and I have had our share of hospital stays in the last few years, but we're not inviting any of you to a pity party. I've discovered that you can always find someone whose troubles are worse than your own.

Tough times? Child stuff compared to what the person who has rejected Christ will experience during the Great Tribulation. I would not want anyone to go through those days. That is the reason I will speak and write until the Lord says, "You've stayed down there long enough, Dale; it's time to come home."

Right now he says to us in his Book: "For our light affliction, which is but for a moment, is working for us a far more exceeding and eternal weight of glory" (2 Cor. 4:17).

Yes, partners, that's good news.

Family Values in a Fractured World

6

> As for me and my house, we will serve the LORD.
>
> Joshua 24:15

WHAT IS A "DYSFUNCTIONAL" family? When we were raising our blended family of different nationalities, we had never heard of the term. Look it up—it means abnormal, impaired, incomplete. Is that the norm in America today?

Dan Quayle struck a raw spot in the American psyche when he started the commotion about family values. Though he stirred up a lot of controversy—just because he spoke the truth about immorality in the entertainment industry—what he had to say was worth hearing. Quayle said, "Despite their differences, families are united by such qualities as responsibility, communication, love and respect, faith and community involvement."[1]

Right on, Dan! The American family may be under attack, but it's not dead.

Family Foes

Roy says, "When the enemies of our freedom under God are successful in breaking up our homes, they have broken our backs—because the home is the backbone of America."

Our backbone is being weakened today by a befuddled society that looks in the wrong places for family values.

Remember when the family hour on television was for families? Broadcasters used to set aside the 8 to 9 P.M. hour as a safe time for children to watch television. *The Brady Bunch,* the wholesome teenagers in *Happy Days,* and *The Cosby Show* were entertainment havens for big and little couch potatoes. However, even the traditional family viewing hour on Sunday nights is now filled with explicit sexual references, off-color language, and violence. I doubt that the stories Roy and I did, where the good guys won over the bad guys, would pass a network's proposal stage. Too goody-two-shoes for today's viewers.

An article in the *Los Angeles Times* stated: "The networks have narrowed their target viewing audience to adults, primarily between the ages of 18 and 49, because advertisers believe they are the key consumers in America."[2]

When it comes to money versus morals, we know what wins.

The Kaiser Foundation funded a report on "Sex and the Mass Media" and concluded that the media's "love affair with sex and romance" contributes to irresponsible sexual behavior among young people, including unplanned and unwanted pregnancies.[3]

Talk shows are so frank that nothing is sacred. It astounds me that people will divulge their sins so openly. Dirty linen should be thrown in the washing machine, not hung out on the lamppost for everyone to see!

What about language? We have become so desensitized to raw and profane words that they don't have an impact anymore. A friend of mine had her office next to a school playground, and she said that the words that came out of the children sounded like those of hardened street thugs.

Network executives claim that they are just reacting to the needs of the marketplace. What is watched sells advertising, they rationalize. Look, the television moguls say, it's the parents who must take responsibility for what their children see. I agree with that, but somehow it doesn't cut to the core of the problem. When good taste and moral values are abdicated, it's everybody's responsibility to change things. Don't the media makers have children too?

The triune god of today is money, sex, and power.

Before Cradle and Grave

What is human life worth? Millions of babies are killed every day by abortions. One of the foremost debates in America is over the rights of a woman to choose to abort and the rights of a child to live. The Bible says: "Your eyes saw my substance, being yet unformed. And in Your book they all were written, The days fashioned for me, When as yet there were none of them" (Ps. 139:16). God knew us in our mother's womb: "Before I formed you in the womb I knew you" (Jer. 1:5). Abortion is one of the greatest crimes in America and should be called what it is . . . murder.

The unborn child has no rights, and the elderly are burdens. We do not want to be saddled with aged parents, so they are farmed out to nursing homes. Many parents also dread being "a burden to their children." What about the burdens we were to them in our childhood? What about the nights our parents lost sleep because of our ailments and fretfulness? Our elderly should be viewed as blessings, not burdens.

Where is the dignity of maturity? Why are we so loathe to age? Why do we spend thousands of dollars on face-lifts, tummy tucks, chin tucks, buttock lifts, and breast implants to try to escape the aging process? As I told a columnist for the *Los Angeles Times* who accused me of having a face-lift, "No, I have not had a face-lift. What's the point? I could lift everything in my body, but inside is the same old mileage."

Every stage of our life is important . . . and, I might add, rewarding.

The New American Family

A typical family is as obsolete as the Edsel. Gone are the days when June Cleaver was in the kitchen with a batch of cookies when the kids came home from school, or Ward Cleaver walked in the front door after an eight-hour day at the office. It is impossible to return to those days.

Today fewer and fewer wives stay home—22 percent, according to the latest census figures, which is a drastic change from 61 percent just thirty years ago. The size of families is smaller, too, with the typical family just 3.2 people. I love that statistic, because I've wondered who that two-tenths of a person could be!

Although I've never been big on statistics, it startled me to read that among first-time mothers under age thirty in America, 40 percent are not married.[4]

As I thought about what is called the "new American family," I realized that Roy's and my own family, four-generational as it is, falls into all of the categories. Divorced, single-parent, career woman, two-career parent, stay-at-home mom—I've been them all. As the old cracker-barrel poet Edgar Guest said, "It takes a heap o' livin' in a house t' make it home." And I guess you could say we've done a heap o' livin'.

Pressure Cooker Families

Carole and I were talking about our early marriage days, and she told me that the only way she knew how to cook then was with a pressure cooker. During World War II, when meat rationing was in effect, her father gave the newlyweds a choice sirloin steak as a present. You guessed it—Carole put it in the pressure cooker. If you know anything about cooking, you know that would turn sirloin into shoe leather.

Today we have good quality men, women, and children who are dumped into this pressure cooker society. No wonder we explode under stress. Our spouses urge us to spend more time with them. Our children tease us to play. Our boss demands we work faster and more efficiently. Our church desires us to be available for committees. Our community pleads for us to be involved with local projects. Television shows, magazines, and billboards implore us to have more money, more power, more sex. People try to do too much and end up neglecting priorities.

This pressure is revealed in the choice of seminars many choose to go to: time management or "How to Organize Your Life." I am not a completely organized person myself but I have learned how to live a pressure cooker life by depending on God's wisdom and power.

Pressure itself is not bad. We would never see a diamond unless a piece of coal had been pressurized. We would never have achievers or champions if there were no pressure. J. Hudson Taylor, missionary to China, said, "As long as the pressure does not come between me and my Savior, but presses me to Him, then the greater the pressure, the greater my dependence upon Him."

Handling pressure does not necessarily mean slowing down. I have known people who accomplish more in less time, simply because they do not major in minors. One minister I know will skip a committee meeting because one of his children is playing in a school game. A couple in a two-career family said they have become "social nerds," turning down most invitations for social functions so they can concentrate on what's more important at this point in their lives.

The problem comes, however, when Christians are too pressured to take their burdens to the Lord. When this happens, we fail to tap into the greatest power source we have. Who would think of having a houseful of electrical appliances and not plugging them in?

We all spend so much time on self-improvement and self-fulfillment that we become self-absorbed. The happiest people I know, even those with pressurized lives, are those who are first God-directed, then others-centered.

All of my life I have been a hurry-up woman. The only way I have slowed down is when the Lord has said, "Stop." And that is more frequent lately. It has given me a chance to think and evaluate some of the lessons of life.

The Buck Stops Here

One thing I've noticed is that we are so quick to blame others for the erosion of family values. One of our favorite targets is the educational system. As I was twirling my pencil over a yellow pad, ready to send some notes to Carole for this chapter, I grabbed my tape recorder instead and began to reminisce.

Shortly after Roy and I were married and living in Hollywood, we became close friends with a woman who was an informant for our government in the days when "communist leanings" were suspected. She lived next door to an internationally known singer whose family leaned toward the left; consequently, she had made interesting observations about inroads this extremely liberal family had made into the school system.

At the PTA meetings our friend, the government agent, attended, our U.S. history books were under attack. The communist sympathizers wanted any hard-won U.S. victories either soft-pedaled or deleted. These people were strong, influential, and vocal. The parents who valued the true record didn't stand up against them and were outnumbered. The erosion began in our history books. We are all at fault for not standing up for our values. We assumed for years that history stood as true and validated and it would always be that way. Not so.

We are getting exactly what we deserve, since we took the easy way of buckling under to those who wanted to alter the American way to their way.

Even teaching methods have contributed to the downgrading of our children's education. Phonics is not the prevalent method to teach reading anymore; rather, in many cases, systems called "whole language" are being used. As a result, we are graduating functionally illiterate students from our schools. Granted, they are far ahead of us in technology, but are they learning to think out a problem or do they simply depend on computers?

Whole books are written about literacy, and that is not my purpose here. But I do want to say that without a generation who can read with understanding, how can we grow and flourish? My hat is off to Barbara Bush and the impetus she gave to the literacy movement. Some of the greatest family values are learned when children are cuddled on their mother's or father's lap with a book in their hands.

Value of a Christian Heritage

In one of our photo albums is a picture of me at age five, sitting before a huge American flag in front of my grandparents' home in Uvalde, Texas. I was taught at an early age to love and respect our flag because of what it stands for. Since I spent a lot of time in Uvalde, I was also taught to respect the Alamo in San Antonio because of the sacrifices made there. Any Texan knows that the rallying cry, "Remember the Alamo!" is a symbol of courage and sacrifice.

My grandfather Wood was my hero. He was a tall, angular Texan and represented to me everything a grandfather should be. He was painfully honest, as the following story will show.

I remember how he insisted that my mother accompany him to the railroad ticket agency to repay what he thought my mother owed. My brother was a sickly child and very small for a five-year-old. He was ill when we traveled by train from Memphis to Uvalde and spent most of the trip sitting on Mama's lap. She didn't buy him a half-price ticket.

"But, Papa, I held him most of the way, and besides, they would never believe he is five years old."

"Daughter," Grandfather Wood said, "we will not defraud the railroad. We are paying for a half ticket."

My mother applied Grandfather's teaching of love for the Lord, honesty, and patriotism to my brother and me. I know the value of the proverb, "Train up a child in the way he should go, And when he is old he will not depart from it" (Prov. 22:6). I was thirty-five and my brother was forty when we returned to the precepts of her teaching, which she had learned at the feet of Grandfather and Grandmother Wood.

Early-taught values really do pay off later.

Grandfather Wood also believed in the free enterprise system. He did not believe in going into debt. He said, "If you have to sell the shirt off your back to pay your debts, you do it." He also believed that bankruptcy was a disgrace.

He was a poor boy with a fourth-grade education, but he educated eight children through college and left a sizable estate at his death.

Although we are new creatures when we become Christians, I also believe that genetic tendencies are important. One of my forefathers was jailed for preaching the gospel instead of adhering to the dictates of the Church of

England. He did street preaching, drawing quite a crowd around him. When he was jailed, he didn't stop. He preached from his jailhouse window to people down below. His genes are strong in me. Since making Jesus Christ my Lord as well as Savior, I believe his heritage is partly responsible for my forthright declaration of Christian faith in the midst of a show business career, even at the expense of a contract.

Building on the Rock

The Lord has told us to build our homes on solid rock. As the old hymn says, "All other ground is sinking sand."

If we have a spiritual heritage, we have a firm foundation to withstand the turmoil around us. We won't be blown away when the storms break loose . . . as they will.

Billy Graham's daughter, Gigi, wrote a delightful book to celebrate Billy and Ruth's golden wedding anniversary. In part of it, though, she soberly observed:

> It is frightening when you think about the lack of family role models today. My children look around them and just shake their heads. They

have been disillusioned again and again when Christian couples and families they had admired and looked up to are shattered by unfaithfulness and divorce.

Where do we look for this Christian heritage we long to pass on to the next generation?[5]

Where *do* we look? We must look to the Lord to build our families. He will never disappoint us. He will never give us bad advice. He will never abandon us. He is our heritage. We have been adopted by him: "You received the Spirit of adoption by whom we cry out, 'Abba, Father.' The Spirit Himself bears witness with our spirit that we are children of God, and if children, then heirs—heirs of God and joint heirs with Christ" (Rom. 8:15–17).

People can write books, give sermons, and make speeches about family values, but we've heard enough of those. In our society that is struggling from blow after blow against our very foundation we need lived-out examples of good family life, not just words.

Every believer has a rich family heritage. If you don't find good examples in your own family, then look to the family of believers down through the generations. Better yet, let your family heritage start with you! Begin today to pass on new values to your children and grandchildren. Hebrews 12 says we are surrounded by a great cloud of witnesses who cheer us on in this endurance race we call life. So how can we lose?

I remember the times when Roy and I rode Trigger and Buttermilk, our horses, in parades. Children would line the sidewalks and cheer wildly as we waved at them along the route. Their enthusiasm was all the encouragement we needed. No wonder Jesus said, "Let the little children come to me." They are fresh vessels, waiting to be filled by someone who will show them God's love.

Grown-ups may make a shambles out of a world God intended to be beautiful, but just when we're ready to give up, along come the children, bright-eyed and eager to learn. We older blunderers take hope and go on with the fight for a new generation.

When I begin to get depressed at the erosion of biblical family values, I realize I must stop and remember that God is in charge. He is able to heal our families with his love.

Value of Friendships

7

There is a friend who sticks closer than a brother.

Proverbs 18:24

A RECENT MOVIE was called *A Few Good Men.* In my life I have been privileged to have many friends, but in every life there are just "a few good friends." Usually, the Lord provides them at just the times we need them most.

Charles Spurgeon was called "the prince of preachers," and his grasp of the Scriptures and deep love for Christ infused his sermons and books, which are quoted in evangelical churches throughout the world. In a book on meditations, he wrote this:

Friendship is the only thing in the world concerning the usefulness of which all mankind are agreed. Friendship seems as necessary an element of a comfortable existence in this world as fire and water, or even air itself. A man may drag along a miserable existence in proud solitary dignity, but his life is scarce life; it is nothing but an existence, the tree of life being stripped of the leaves of hope and the fruits of joy. *He who would be happy here must have friends; and he who would be happy hereafter must above all things, find a friend in the world to come, in the person of God, the Father of His people* (author's italics).[1]

Why Some People Don't Have Friends

One of the most friendless men in America was also one of the richest men in the world. In his later years, Howard Hughes led a life of such lunacy that most of us could not understand. His physical appearance became so bizarre that he must have been repulsive to all of the people who were paid to care for him. His beard hung down to his waist, and his fingernails were like claws. Hughes was only interested in airplanes, technology, and making money. There were no great eulogies when he died.

Some people don't have friends because they are so caught up in the superficial life of parties, social engagements, and work that they don't take time to cultivate deep, lasting friendships. It's been said that God gave us things to use and people to enjoy. People without friends use people and enjoy things.

Some people don't have friends because qualities in their personalities are objectionable. Too loud. Too manipulating. Too critical. Too sarcastic. Too self-pitying. Perhaps we all have one or more of those traits at some time. But they sure don't need to be permanent.

Just consider some of Jesus' followers. James and John, the sons of Zebedee, were selfish and wanted to sit next to Jesus in places of honor. They did not endear themselves to the other ten disciples any more than the person who shoves ahead of us in line. Peter might have destroyed a precious friendship when he denied knowing Jesus. Nathanael was sarcastic. "Can anything good come out of Nazareth?" (John 1:46). Saul was brutal and ruthless before he met Christ on the road to Damascus. Mark skipped out on his friends and went home without an explanation.

Whenever someone says, "That's just the way I am," wait. Remember, you don't have to stay in a ditch just because you fell in it.

"When someone becomes a Christian he becomes a brand new person inside. He is not the same any more. A new life has begun!" (2 Cor. 5:17 LB).

To Be a Friend . . . and Have Friends

While we were writing this chapter, dancer Gene Kelly died. To Sherman White, a soundman who worked on Kelly's films, his death meant more than a loss of a great talent. It was the passing of a man who knew the value of friendship.

"Gene was a great fella," White told a reporter. "He was everybody's friend. He was just the guy next door, except he had a tremendous talent."

White ended the interview by adding, "If you have real, great, honest-to-God character, like Jimmy Stewart or Gene Kelly, you go out gracefully."[2]

Ralph Waldo Emerson said, "The only reward of virtue is virtue; the only way to have a friend is to be one."

Many today don't know how to be a friend. To be a friend, we should dare to say, "I love you." Some people choke on those words as if they were cod liver oil. Love is the basis of all friendships, and without it we only have people who gallop through our lives without stopping to graze and enjoy the view. Why do we need to have principles and guidelines for relationships that should be as natural as breathing? Perhaps it's because we have been programmed to "look out for number one." Howard Hughes did that, and look where it got him.

Carole told me about a business seminar she attended where the main speaker broke down on stage after telling a story about his father. For the first time in that man's life, his father told him that he loved him. The man was fifty-seven years old. My parents never ceased to tell me they loved me, no matter how wayward I was. Jesus never ceases to love me, just as I am. When we sing, "What a friend I have in Jesus," we're singing about the ultimate friendship. Jesus is our example of real love. He has said, "I love you," in countless ways.

To be a friend, be cautious in criticism. When someone says, "This is for your own good," I wonder what good will come of it. D. L. Moody was a great evangelist and preacher. One of his famous sayings was, "Right now I'm having so much trouble with D. L. Moody that I don't have time to find fault with the other fellow."

Years ago I wrote a book called *My Spiritual Diary*. When you write a book, appear before an audience, or have a position of influence in any field, you will be criticized. It's been said that the farther up the ladder you climb, the easier it is for people to take potshots at you. One day I wrote this story in that diary:

> Our good friends, Dr. Norman Vincent Peale, and Frank Mead and Wilbur Davies of the Fleming Revell Company have just left. What a delightful time we had together. We talked of the trials and tribulations of being a Christian in these days and we had a good laugh over a lot of them. These men have a great sense of humor. They can laugh off the most devastating criticism of their books and sermons, and that is a gift straight from God! They are serious enough when the criticism is important, but stupid or intolerant criticism they throw off like so many ducks shedding water off their backs. I cherish the gift of good humor in the faith. There would be a lot fewer spiritual casualties if we had more of it.

We discussed the problem of publishing religious books—of how hard it is to get a book published that will find any audience at all, with people in the churches so divided and quarreling among themselves.

Dr. Peale has the answer, I think. He says, "Write what God gives you to write, and forward all letters of criticism to Him!"[3]

Wouldn't it be great to hand over criticism to the Lord instead of letting it fester in our hearts? Someone once said that constructive criticism is when I criticize you. Destructive criticism is when you criticize me.

To be a friend, be an encourager. When Robin died, the floodgates of care and encouragement opened. The Eilers family—Frances, Leonard, and Joy—came to the house and waited until Robin's little body was taken away and stayed with me and let me cry. I'm so grateful they didn't say, "Now, now, don't cry." They put their arms around me and let me pour it all out. That's friendship.

Some people are just natural encouragers, it seems. They send a note of congratulation or consolation. They bring food when you can't cook for yourself. They keep quiet when you need to talk.

Rich DeVos, cofounder of the Amway corporation, with twelve thousand employees and two million distributors, was asked, "How do you lead such a vast organization?" DeVos answered, "Oh, I'm not a leader; I'm just a cheerleader."

Good friends are good encouragers, but the greatest encouragement of all is in the Book. "For everything that was written in the past was written to teach us, so that through endurance and the *encouragement of the Scriptures we might have hope*" (Rom. 15:4 NIV, emphasis added).

Friends accept us just as we are. This does not mean they approve of everything. Acceptance is a different matter. When I hear the song, "Just As I Am" sung as an invitation, I know that God hasn't asked us to clean up our act before we accept him. Good friends see our shortcomings and love us anyhow.

The Bible says, "Therefore encourage one another and build each other up" (1 Thess. 5:11 NIV).

The Power in a Touch

A friend can boost your day with a pat on the back or a hug. I believe we all need at least eight hugs a day. The way to get them is to give them. Hugs between friends are a way of saying, "You're special to me," "I've missed you," or "We both need a boost."

We wither without the touch of caring hands. A computer instructor was teaching a class on the use of the more sophisticated methods of accessing information. He bragged about the prowess of his three-year-old daughter, who knew how to turn on a computer and find special pictures and games she could play by herself. Her father said, "She's learning to read by CD-ROM." What happens to the wonderful closeness that comes when a child sits on Daddy's or Mommy's lap and is read to from books? Computers cannot cuddle or hug.

Jesus used the power of touch to cure a man of leprosy, to raise Peter's mother-in-law from her sickbed, to take the children in his arms. The touch of Jesus can touch and heal anyone. It did me.

Friends Listen

A psychiatrist said that patients come to his office because they know so few people who will genuinely listen to what they are saying. Good listeners listen with their eyes, not just their ears. When someone looks around the room or glances sideways to make sure he doesn't miss someone more important, you know he isn't listening. I have often heard in my life, "Grandma, watch me." We are not listening unless we are watching.

Alan Loy McGinnis, in his book *The Friendship Factor,* tells a story about Lincoln during the darkest hours of the Civil War. The president sent for an old friend and fellow lawyer to come to Washington because he wanted to discuss some problems.

The friend, Leonard Swett, hurried to the White House, and Lincoln talked to him for hours about the arguments pro and con for freeing the slaves. Lincoln did all the talking himself. Swett went back to Illinois without even giving his opinion. All Lincoln wanted was a friendly, sympathetic listener.

For thirty years we have had a friend who has listened to many of our joys and triumphs. He is Bill Hansen, the minister of our church. When we first moved to Apple Valley, we visited the church where he preached to see if we liked it. Bill was never without a smile. I thought, *Is this just a façade?* So I went back again. His smile was always there and it was real. That smile and his listening ear have sustained us through many experiences.

Jesus was a great conversationalist, but he was also a very attentive listener. He asked questions of Roman officers, blind men, rabbis, fishermen, mothers, religious zealots, rich people, common people. We call him a Great Teacher, but he was also a Great Listener.

Friends Share Joys and Sorrows

I received a wedding invitation that said, "This day I will marry my friend, the one I laugh with, dream with, love . . ." Isn't that great? I wish more people would fall in friend before they fall in love. Roy and I had a friendship that grew into love. I believe friendship is the basic ingredient for a good marriage.

Women have more close friends than men, and I've often wondered why. Little girls walk to school together holding hands and say, "She's my best friend." Little boys punch and cuff each other as a sign of friendship. Girls love to have slumber parties and tell secrets. Boys like to go into the woods and play "search and rescue." When they grow up, the same trend continues. Women's friendships revolve around sharing; men's revolve around activities.

When I was making pictures at Republic Studios, I had a double, Alice Van. When there was a long shot on a horse, Alice rode. She took some of my falls for me. Alice was a world-championship trick rider and the first woman to acquire a horse-training license in the state of Illinois. During the time we worked together, we both had sons who lived with our parents. We had a lot in common.

Alice and I are still close friends. She is like a sister to me. No matter how far away we may live, when we get together it's like yesterday. Friendships like that are not developed overnight.

Memories of good friends never fade. My agent, Art Rush, has gone to be with the Lord, but I shall never forget his friendship. When our dearest Debbie was killed in the school bus accident and Roy was seriously ill in the hospital, all of the arrangements were left to me. Art was there, helping me make decisions, doing all of the little chores that needed to be done. He never asked, "What can I do?" He just did them.

When I talk about my friends, I wonder how people can manage without friends of their own. The only thing that has sustained me has been my wonderful friend Jesus and those precious people he has brought into my life.

An unknown poet wrote these words:

When trouble comes your soul to try,
You love the friend who just stands by.
Perhaps there's nothing he can do;
The thing is strictly up to you,
For there are troubles all your own,
And paths the soul must tread alone;
Times when love can't smooth the road,
Nor friendship lift the heavy load.

But just to feel you have a friend,
Who will stand by until the end;
Whose sympathy through all endures,
Whose warm handclasp is always yours.
It helps somehow to pull you through,
Although there's nothing he can do;
And so with fervent heart we cry,
"God bless the friend who just stands by."[4]

The Bible says: "A friend loves at all times" (Prov. 17:17 NIV).

Value of Discipline

8

Blessed is the man you discipline, O LORD.
Psalm 94:12 NIV

GOD HAS DISCIPLINED ME for the past thirty-five years. I admit I haven't enjoyed being taken to the woodshed. However, I know that without his discipline I would be like one of those little windup toys that spins and spins out of control.

In Eugene Peterson's paraphrase of the Bible, the writer of Hebrews reminds us:

So don't feel sorry for yourselves. Or have you forgotten how good parents treat children, and that God regards you as *his* children?

"My dear child, don't shrug off God's
    discipline,
  but don't be crushed by it either.
It's the child he loves that he disciplines;
    the child he embraces, he also corrects."

God is educating you; that's why you must never
drop out. He's treating you as dear children. This
trouble you're in isn't punishment, it's *training,*
the normal experience of children. Only irresponsible parents leave children to fend for themselves. Would you prefer an irresponsible God?
(Heb. 12:5–7)[1]

In the past few decades, personal discipline
seems to have taken a backseat to "do your own
thing." Frank Sinatra had his eightieth birthday
recently. A special celebration was held in a large
theater and televised for millions. It seemed to
me that the biggest and longest ovation was for
his rendition of "My Way." When Sinatra sings,
"I did it my way," he brings out our independent spirit. It's the child in us who says, "Please,
Mother, let me do it myself."

For a Christian, discipline or self-control
means we choose God's way instead of insist-
ing on having our own way.

Many times I've stood in church and sung, "Take my life, and let it be consecrated Lord to Thee." Through the hymn we continue to give our moments, our hands, our feet, our voice, our lips, our intellect, our will, our heart, our love, and, finally, ourselves. That's a tall order. If we give our lives to Jesus Christ, he has the right to discipline us his way.

Enemies of Discipline

Laziness and emotionalism are two of the greatest enemies of discipline. Lazy people can't be bothered to acquire disciplined habits in life. A friend of mine has a big card on her refrigerator that says, "Procrastination is the thief of success." We often fall into the Scarlett O'Hara complex: "I'll think about it tomorrow."

If an athlete puts off training because she is tired, she could lose in the competition. If a businessman doesn't answer phone calls, he might find himself without clients. If an actress parties all night and doesn't learn her lines, she's out of a job. If a student doesn't study, he will flunk.

The principle of self-discipline is this: "Do what needs to be done when it ought to be done, whether you like it or not."

Disciplining ourselves is often difficult because we take on the whole task all at once, get discouraged, and give up. But if we took just one step at a time, we'd soon know the sweetness of success. For example, in writing a book, I put one word at a time on the page. In studying a script, I can only memorize one side (a half page) at a time. And a marathon racer takes one mile at a time.

Emotional people who live by their feelings also struggle with self-discipline. To say, "Well, I'll do it if I feel like it," is the opposite of a disciplined life. With that attitude we would only read the Bible and pray when we felt like it. We would go to church only on the days we felt like it. But if we only went to work on the days we felt like it, we would not keep a job. Should we give our Lord any less service than we give our earthly employer?

When Robin was alive, I developed self-discipline by necessity. I was working five and six days a week and had a home and family to manage. To discipline myself to find time alone was important for my sanity. I did a lot of praying in my car and between scenes on the set. I learned to talk less, which for a woman who loves to gab is a real challenge.

Today I have to discipline myself because my health is not very good. I need to stretch and do my exercises every morning and night. When Carole called to ask me some questions about this subject, she said, "What is the most difficult area of your life to discipline?" That caught me off guard. I said, "It's trying not to become irritated when I get constant interruptions."

It was quiet on the other end of the line. "Do you mean like this phone call?"

We had a good laugh.

Luck Is a Loser

Joy Eilers is a dear friend who has accompanied me on the piano for many television programs. She plays so effortlessly that she makes it look easy. Some might say, "I wish I could play like Joy." They don't mean it, though. If they did, they would have practiced every day since they were a child, even when they didn't feel like it.

We call people "natural" athletes, but these talents come from hours and years of training.

Take away the discipline of mind and body from an athlete and you have a loser.

Success has its price.

The Dennis Byrd story is an inspiring example of discipline and determination. From the time he was a child, Dennis wanted to play football. He finally made it as one of the game's leading defensive linemen with the New York Jets. During one game, he collided with a 280-pound teammate, and his neck was broken.

Doctors said he would be paralyzed from the neck down for life. But they underestimated Dennis and his personal relationship with Jesus. In the grueling weeks of rehabilitation, which took more discipline than football training ever did, Dennis defied the negative prognosis and walked out of the hospital. Today he is coaching high school football in Oklahoma.

Hold Your Horses

We were in St. Louis for a rodeo sponsored by the firemen of that city. When Roy galloped into the arena and Trigger saluted the crowd by standing on his rear legs, the place went wild. How many hours of disciplined training do you think it took to perfect that trick? I can't even guess. Horses are like children—they will run wild if not disciplined.

We have had many dogs, and Roy spent untold hours training them to be good hunters. Now that we are unable to make the effort to discipline dogs, we own cats. If anyone knows the method to discipline a cat, please give me the secret. You don't own cats; they own you.

If we discipline our pets, should we do any less with our children? Should God do any less with his children?

Train Up a Child

When someone mentions discipline, most people think of children. Perhaps it is because that is where discipline should start. Undisciplined adults were undoubtedly undisciplined children.

When we were living in Encino, California, it was my habit to do one big shopping trip every two weeks. Dodie was about two years old when we went on one of these major expeditions. (Dear mothers, I know what it is like to shop with children in tow. It takes courage.)

Our cart was groaning with groceries, and Dodie was perched in the seat in the front of the basket. She began to demand chewing gum in a tone loud enough for the butcher in the back of the store to hear. I said "no," and she raised her voice another decibel. Actually, she was howling. I lifted her out of the cart, put her over my leg, and gave her a few choice whacks on her backside. Then I put her back in the seat and proceeded through the checkout line. Every parent who has ever had to discipline a child in a public place knows the feeling. You want to be invisible until your child is a perfect little cherub.

A lady shopper (probably a Dr. Spock follower) said so I could hear, "I've never seen anything so disgusting in my life."

I smiled and answered, "I'll bet she'll never do it again." And she didn't.

A pastor in Santa Barbara caused a stir of controversy by suggesting that the best way to prevent young children from joining gangs is an old-fashioned spanking. Reverend Richard Ramos works with a group that deals with drug prevention. He was quoted as saying, "I know this isn't going to make me popular with some parents . . . but this is one father who does not believe that spanking my children is an act of violence."

Ramos suggested spanking two- to ten-year-olds for open defiance or to punish them for having a rebellious attitude. He also recommended spanking before the parent gets angry, using one to three swats with the hand on the buttocks only, and spanking hard enough that the child remembers or cries.[2]

Where were you, Reverend Ramos, when I was in the grocery store with Dodie?

Ann Landers answers letters from her readers with a lot of wisdom. One woman wrote about visiting a state park and stopping to take pictures of her six-year-old daughter and two-year-old son standing next to two life-size dinosaur models. These giant figures were roped off and signs proclaimed, Do Not Touch the Models. Other families were there with their children, who were going under the ropes and climbing on the models to pose for pictures.

The behavior of the children who were allowed to do what they wanted, in spite of warning signs, infuriated the letter writer. She said in a loud voice to her husband, "What good children we have, honey! They can't read the posters, but they know that a rope means 'Do not touch.'" The other parents gave her ugly looks and continued to take pictures.

The writer also told about going to a restaurant where children at a nearby table were spitting drinks at each other through straws, getting those at the writer's table wet. The parents ignored complaints and said, "They're just having fun, nothing personal."

Landers was asked, "What are these parents teaching their children?"

Her reply was: "Those parents are teaching their children it's OK to ignore signs posted for their own safety, and if it's fun to do something, go ahead and do it, even though it interferes with the comfort or well-being of others. I pity those children. They are starting out in life with a lot of baggage. It's going to be a rough journey."[3]

When our children were young, we disciplined them with spankings and when they were older, by withdrawing privileges. Our children knew without a shadow of a doubt that we loved them. In later years Dusty said, "Mom, you ruined our discipline by saying you were sorry. You had to discipline us. We needed it."

If I ruined their discipline, the results don't show it. They turned out real good.

I frequently misbehaved as a child. (That's a conservative statement!) I knew what a spanking meant but I also knew that my parents would be merciful when they saw any sign of repentance.

One time I was told to help my little brother throw some bricks over a fence in our backyard. That wasn't my idea of fun; I wanted to play with my dolls. In a fit of defiance, I threw a brick that hit the fence and bounced back on my brother's head. The blood rushed out of a deep gash in his forehead. I ran screaming into the house, "I've killed my little brother!"

Mama and Daddy came out running, applied a bandage to Hillman, and called the doctor. I fully expected a whipping. I didn't mean to hurt him, and my parents knew it, so they let discipline take care of itself.

Proper Discipline Is Not Abuse

Our nation is full of horrific stories of child abuse. In my book *Hear the Children Crying*, I said, "I firmly believe that it is sometimes almost impossible for a parent to know where to draw the line between punishment and abuse, unless that parent has a strong religious faith."[4]

Discipline must always be done with love and never in the heat of anger. A child must know the boundaries of good and bad conduct and know the consequences of stepping out of those boundaries (just as the children who ducked under the ropes around the dinosaurs should have been pulled back by their parents).

Even an animal is safer and happier with a loving master to train him.

The permissiveness of the past is reaping the criminals of the present. When Dr. James Dobson was asked to define "permissiveness," he said, "I refer to the absence of effective parental authority, resulting in the lack of boundaries for the child. This word represents childish disrespect, defiance, and the general confusion that occurs in the absence of adult leadership."[5]

It has been said that it is less painful to discipline a child than to weep over a spoiled youth.

Which will we choose, Americans: discipline or despair?

9 Value of Patience

My brethren, count it all joy when you fall into various trials, knowing that the testing of your faith produces patience.

James 1:2–3

TERI HAD A FRANTIC DAY. Her second-grader had missed the bus, and she had to take her to school. No time to dress, so she went in her bathrobe, buckled the baby in his car seat (dirty diaper and all), and arrived just as the bell rang. The president of the PTA spied her and rushed over to the car to talk. Teri had to roll down the window and reveal her charming image and the interior of the odor-filled car.

The day continued to deteriorate.

The sink overflowed when she answered the phone and forgot to turn off the water.

The baby wouldn't take a nap.

Her oldest child came home with a D in geometry and slammed the door so hard that the crystal vase on the shelf fell off and scattered glass on the hall floor.

The cat got a sliver of glass in his paw and howled until Teri got the tweezers to pull it out. That ungrateful cat scratched her hand.

Milk spilled, cookies burned, phone rang, supper was unplanned. One look in the mirror confirmed that this was a bad hair day.

Teri slumped in a kitchen chair to write a grocery list at 5 P.M. and prayed the great American prayer: "Lord, give me patience . . . right now."

No one's life is the same as another's, but I can empathize with a day like Teri's. It seems as if I put too much on my platter every day. I cram too much into a crowded schedule and then want it done yesterday. I get antsy inside and feel like I'm being pushed. The person who is pushing, however, is looking at me in the mirror.

When a child wants Christmas or her birthday to come tomorrow, we say, "Be patient."

When someone honks the horn for us to hurry, we mutter, "Why can't he be patient?"

Patience is a virtue, but for many of us it does not come easily.

Wait Here

One of the hardest lessons to learn in life is patience. Waiting for a child in the high chair to eat may be an endurance contest. To listen without interrupting to the stories of a long-winded friend or someone who details every scene from a movie qualifies us for sainthood.

To "wait upon the Lord," though, may be the greatest test of patience given to us.

During Robin's short lifetime, I was asked by many magazine editors to write an article about what it was like to have a child with Down's syndrome. I promised the Lord and those editors that someday I would. "When the time is right."

The day after Robin's funeral, I was looking at her lovely little face in a picture on my desk. I was dazed and numb with grief. Endless calls of sympathy came from our friends, which provided some distraction from the ache inside me.

Suddenly, thoughts came into my mind so fast that I picked up a pencil and started to write. My hand finally became cramped, and I couldn't write anymore.

Roy and I had contracted months before to do a dramatic program for Dodge Motors on NBC and shortly afterwards a show in Madison Square Garden. When I wasn't on mike and had a few moments to rest, I thought about Robin's story. Why couldn't I continue it? I closed my eyes and started to pray, and the answer came so clearly, *Let Robin write it.* I was letting my feelings, my grief, interfere with the message. *Let her speak for herself and others who are handicapped like she was.*

I picked up a pen again and began to write every waking moment. On the train to New York I wrote and wrote. By the time we pulled into Grand Central Station, the little book was finished. It had been just six weeks since Robin went to be with the Lord.

Now what do I do, Lord?

I wasn't really sure of my direction; it was just the echo of my heartbreak that drove me. I took my notes and walked over to Central Park and sat on a stone bench next to the zoo. Patience, Dale, patience.

I bowed my head and just kept saying over and over, "Thy will be done, thy will be done. Please tell me if this is of you, Lord. Please tell me."

When I looked up, I saw a woman coming toward me with a Down's syndrome little girl. I knew that God had spoken to me, because at that time people didn't take those children out for public view. I fairly ran back to the hotel and burst into our suite. "Roy, he did it! God spoke to me about Robin's book!"

Dear, patient Roy had suffered as much as I had over Robin's death, but he sustained and supported me in my weakness.

I pulled together all the scraps of paper I had written in the past few weeks. Out of those tearstained notes that I had finished on the train came a little book . . . *Angel Unaware*. It was Robin's book and God's book, not mine. I was merely the hand he used. Now what do I do with it, Lord?

Again, it was as if the Lord directed me to pick up the phone and call Marble Collegiate Church and ask for an appointment with Dr. Norman

Vincent Peale. He had written a chapter in his book *Guide to Confident Living* on "How to Meet Sorrow." When I read it, I thought that someday I wanted to thank him.

As secretaries are prone to do, she told me how busy he was, how people made appointments weeks ahead, etcetera. Fifteen minutes later I walked into his office. This time God hadn't told me to wait.

Dr. Peale was a kind and wise man. We prayed together on our knees, and then I read to him what God had directed me to write. He didn't say a word all through the reading. When I finished, he looked at me with tears in his eyes and said, "It's beautiful. I will help you get it published."

My impatient nature had been bridled until I learned to wait on the Lord's direction.

Patience When Nothing Seems to Be Happening

Sometimes we pray and wait and nothing happens. Why does God take so long? Satan, in the subtle way he can use, begins to play with our thoughts. We begin to condemn ourselves.

Maybe I don't deserve an answer. Doubts begin to cloud our thinking.

Maybe God hasn't heard me. Impatience overwhelms us.

I've waited so long, maybe God just wants me to go ahead and solve this problem on my own. Ego and pride dominate us.

With instant credit, fast food, freeways, jet travel, and now cyberspace, we in America are not prone to patience. Yet the Word of God has a lot to say about waiting.

When Pharaoh of Egypt died, the children of Israel groaned and cried because they wanted out of their slavery. Forty years later, God sent Moses to lead them out of Egypt.

Samuel anointed David king when David was just a boy, but it was another ten or fifteen years before he was finally crowned.

Jesus was twelve years old when he stayed in the temple, asking and answering questions. When he was found by his parents, he returned to Nazareth, and eighteen years passed before he began his public ministry.

We are so impatient to have everything happen *right now*.

Isaiah's words help me realize that God is not punishing us by making us wait; rather, God's timing is gracious. "Therefore the LORD will wait, that He may be gracious to you; and therefore He will be exalted, that He may have mercy on you. For the LORD is a God of justice; blessed are all those who wait for Him" (Isa. 30:18).

God's Stretching

One of my favorite devotionals is Oswald Chambers' *My Utmost for His Highest*. Chambers died in 1917 at the age of forty-three but he still speaks to millions today. Every time I pick up his little book, I marvel that one person could have such insight into the deep truths of the Word. When I nestle into my recliner, with our cat on my lap and Chambers' book in my hand, it's like exploring the deep things of God with an old friend. He writes:

> Patience is more than endurance. A saint's life is in the hands of God like a bow and arrow in the hands of an archer. God is aiming at something the saint cannot see, and He stretches and strains, and every now and again the saint says—"I can-

not stand any more." God does not heed. He goes on stretching till His purpose is in sight, then He lets fly. Trust yourself in God's hands. For what have you need of patience just now? Maintain your relationship to Jesus Christ by the *patience of faith.* "Though He slay me, yet will I wait for Him."[1]

Most of us have seen enough cowboy and Indian movies or watched *Robin Hood* to know how far back the archer pulls the bow before letting go. If the bow could talk, it might say, "Ouch, I've had enough . . . let me loose." Many times in my life I've felt like shouting, *Enough is enough! I can't take any more of this pain!*

When I had my most severe heart attack, it felt like knives were piercing my body. I cried, "Lord, was it like this for you on the cross?" Then I remembered that the Bible said he "endured the cross" (Heb. 12:2).

Endurance is the most intense form of patience.

Waiting Isn't Easy

Anyone who has flown enough to accumulate thousands of those frequent flyer miles knows the frustrations you can encounter at an airport or aboard the plane. We've been in scenes like these. The plane is two hours late. People are grumpy and some are downright mad, letting everyone else know how they feel. Flight attendants are apologizing and trying to keep a positive attitude. When we are finally in the sky, a baby is screaming from the pressure. The meal is late and less than palatable. The lady next to us has a cold and is wearing heavy perfume. The movie has embarrassing scenes, and we worry about the children who are watching.

It's times like these that no one cares if I've written Christian books or have appeared in the movies. All they see is how we react. Are we calm? Smiling? Without irritation?

Did we remember that "the fruit of the Spirit is love, joy, peace, *patience*..." (Gal. 5:22 NIV)?

David was not always a patient man. In Psalm 69 he wrote: "Save me, O God! For the waters have come up to my neck. I sink in deep mire, Where there is no standing; I have come into deep waters, Where the floods overflow me. I am weary with my crying; My throat is dry; My eyes fail while I wait for my God" (vv. 1–3).

It certainly sounds as if David was in trouble. Later on he wrote, "Hear me speedily" (v. 17). Again, in Psalm 70 he pleaded, "Make haste, O God, to deliver me! Make haste to help me, O LORD!" (v. 1).

Isn't it gratifying to know that the great King David was just like us? "Hurry up, God, I'm tired of waiting!"

And yet God says to us:

> But those who wait on the LORD shall renew their strength; they shall mount up with wings like eagles, they shall run and not be weary, they shall walk and not faint (Isa. 40:31).

(My favorite verse.)

Teach Me, Lord, to Wait for Your Power

When Debbie and her girlfriend were killed in that church bus crash in 1964, I needed the Lord's super-spiritual strength. Roy was hospitalized from a spinal fusion. He had been dangerously ill and was in no shape to help with the details of the funeral. To top it off, the press monopolized my phone, and I couldn't even get through to Roy in the hospital.

Debbie's death, Roy's illness, the decisions that had to be made, the pressure of the news media all dealt me a wallop.

I prayed that I would be a witness to the power of the Lord before the people attending the funeral. The Holy Spirit sustained me. God helped me keep my composure in front of all those people. Of course, I fell apart later, but when I needed the strength, he was there.

The Least Dramatic Value

Patience is not very popular today. We feel that the faster we go, the more we accomplish. It seems to be almost a virtue to say, "I'm so busy." We are determined to push everything at breakneck speed.

Roy and I have had a lot of animals during our lifetime. When we get a puppy, it seems like no time before he's grown. A cute little kitten becomes an independent cat in a few months. A baby, on the other hand, takes many years before reaching maturity. Humans take much longer to grow up. God did not design for us to be microwave men and women.

God's work is never hurried. James says, "Let patience have its perfect work" (1:4).

We cannot teach the value of patience in the classroom or from the pulpit. I can write about its value, but they will only be hollow words. Patience is taught in our lives and in our actions.

St. Francis of Assisi wrote: "No one will ever know the full depth of his capacity for patience and humility as long as nothing bothers him. It is only when times are troubled and difficult that he can see how much of either is in him." As the phone interrupts my thoughts again (why don't I have the fortitude to let it ring?), I think, *Oh Lord, teach me to be patient. Right now!*

A Call to Valor

Now it came to pass, when the time had come for Him to be received up, that He steadfastly set His face to go to Jerusalem.

Luke 9:51

JESUS KNEW what awaited him at his destination. Mocking, beatings, human cruelty in the extreme. Then, finally, death by crucifixion. Nevertheless, "He steadfastly set His face to go to Jerusalem."

His was the ultimate example of valor.

Courage is exhibited in many ways. Martyrs have shown physical courage that most of us in America cannot comprehend. Stories from the Nazi death camps stagger us with the degree of man's inhumanity to man. From political prisoners in communist Russia to tortured Christians in Red China, the torment has been beyond what most of us can fathom.

Have we ceased to pray for our suffering brothers and sisters in other parts of the world? We feel so safe inside our churches. The Berlin Wall has fallen. Communism is dead. (Is it?) China has opened its doors to American business and trade. What have we to worry about?

Charles Colson wrote that the Muslim government in Sudan has made it a crime to convert to Christianity. In Sudan, Libya, and other Islamic countries, thousands of women from Christian families have been raped, sold as servants or concubines. Men have been crucified.

Here is a list of places where Christians *today* are being persecuted: Pakistan, Egypt, Saudi Arabia, Iran. There may be more. Colson said,

> Despite the gruesome evidence, the U.S. government inexplicably refuses to recognize what is happening . . . the Immigration and Naturalization Service often denies asylum to victims of anti-Christian terror. The INS even returns them to the countries they have fled—where they face imprisonment, torture, even death—in clear vio-

lation of U.S. laws granting asylum to religious refugees.[1]

Our nation was founded by religious believers fleeing persecution. Have we forgotten? Have we learned anything from history? Remember when our American leaders denied there was religious persecution by communist governments? Then Aleksandr Solzhenitsyn's writings were smuggled out of Russia, and the horror of the Gulag Archipelago was revealed. Perhaps some literary genius will wake us up to Islam-inspired terror.

It doesn't take much valor on our part to raise our voices and take up our pens in defense of fellow believers. If we don't stand up for what we believe, we may fall into that indifferent and lukewarm attitude Jesus condemned in the church at Laodicea. He said, "I know your works, that you are neither cold nor hot. I could wish you were cold or hot. So then, because you are lukewarm, and neither cold nor hot, I will spew you out of My mouth" (Rev. 3:15–16).

I would rather be called a firebrand than a wet noodle.

In small ways and large, people of valor set examples that give us courage. Their stories are more inspiring than the lifestyles of the rich and famous.

When Moses handed over the leadership of Israel to Joshua, he said, "Be strong and of good courage, do not fear nor be afraid of them; for the LORD your God, He is the One who goes with you. He will not leave you nor forsake you" (Deut. 31:6).

God speaks to us today and says, "Be strong and of good courage. I will not leave you."

Left for Dead

Korea has forty-three million people, and more than eleven million are professing Christians. Some of the largest churches in the world are located in South Korea. How did Christianity make such a big impact on a country that is predominantly Buddhist? More than anyone else, one man showed the courage to be persecuted for his faith and light the spark of revival.

When the Communists occupied Korea (1950–53), North Korean soldiers began murdering any civilians who disagreed with communist ideology. Dr. Kim saw his father and his wife brutally killed before his eyes. He was beaten by a club and almost had his throat cut with a sword. He was stuffed into a sack to be thrown into the sea from the top of a cliff, but he was miraculously spared at the last minute.

After the war, Kim felt he was called to preach and managed to travel to the United States to study at Fuller Theological Seminary in California. The rest of the story is the astounding history of the formation of Korea Campus Crusade for Christ under the leadership of Dr. Kim. It has been said that he is the key person in the evangelization of Korea, and today there are Korean Christians all over the world who trace their spiritual origin to him.

God's man in Korea could have been thrown over a cliff in a sack.

God's Smuggler

Brother Andrew is a Dutchman who smuggled Bibles behind the Iron Curtain when the penalty for such an act was imprisonment, even death. He experienced fear, just as all of us do. He wrote,

> I've driven toward the Iron Curtain with my carload of Scripture, arrived at the border, seen the

133

controls, and gotten so scared I've turned around
and driven back to a hotel in the nearest village
where I could pray and fast. I'd stay there until I
had faith that with God I was a majority; and that
I could cross over with Scripture and preach on
the other side and not be caught.[2]

Brother Andrew and his Open Doors ministry
have smuggled millions of Bibles into Russia,
China, parts of Asia, Africa, Central America,
and, finally, the Middle East.

I've never smuggled Bibles or been tortured
for Christ, but I've often wondered if we American Christians will ever be called on to face
that kind of opposition to our faith.

What More Can Be Said about Billy?

The most admired and respected Christian
leader in the world is Billy Graham. He is a man
of valor because he is committed to the purity
and power of his ministry. Billy has faced death
threats, criticism, loneliness, family problems,
and financial insecurity. Yet he has never wavered
from the task God has called him to do.

In spite of his robust appearance on the
podium in front of thousands of people, his

most brutal adversary has probably been his poor health. To list the number of ailments he has suffered would look like a page from a first-year medical student's textbook. (I'm not sure of that analogy, because I've never seen a medical student's textbook.) However, he said, "I intend to keep on going, preaching the gospel, writing the gospel, as long as I have any breath. I hope my last word as I am dying—whether by a bullet wound, by cancer, a heart attack, or a stroke—I hope my dying word will be *Jesus*."[3]

In a call to valor, Billy would be on the front lines.

Stand Up, Stand Up for Jesus

Compromise is the opposite of valor. When we are tempted to compromise our faith, it's like Peter denying Christ three times. Christ forgave him and welcomed him back into his inner circle. But I don't believe Peter ever forgot the humiliation of hearing that cock crow.

Yes, I have compromised. I'm just a sinner saved by grace and have had to ask for forgiveness many times. Although I do not want to elevate myself into the same stratosphere as many uncompromising and courageous souls who have been my heroes, I do remember times when God has given me strength to stand up for what I believe.

Roy and I had signed a contract in 1952 to appear in Madison Square Garden. The show was to go on only three weeks after Robin died. Roy and I rode Trigger and Buttermilk into the center of the arena and sang "Peace in the Valley." It took the power of God's peace to get me through that number. Roy had arranged for the arena to be darkened except for a single shaft of light in the form of a huge cross beaming on us as we sang. It was one of those "moments in time."

The manager of Madison Square Garden had a fit. The whole presentation was "too religious," and the cross was offensive.

Roy said, "You will either leave it in or you will find a new cowboy."

A matinee performance was scheduled for the next day, and hundreds of young people were there. When the cross hit the black turf, the place went wild. The kids stamped and cheered until we thought the bleachers would break.

After the show, the manager said, "Okay, leave the cross in."

Another time we did a variety show that was filmed in Seattle. Ralph Carmichael and his orchestra backed us. In one of my numbers, I sang, "When Christ shall come with shout of acclamation."

When the dress rehearsal ended, the producer of the show said, "Tell Dale she has to take out 'Christ.'"

I said, "I will not take Christ out."

The show was canceled after two or three times, and our contract was not renewed. It was too late in the season to get another contract, so we were out of work.

Extremists, Etc.

In football and baseball stadiums, zeal for the sport makes perfect sense. Stand, yell, scream, it's okay. But stand up for God and you'll be labeled. "Right-wing religious extremist" is the latest in name-calling. A little bit of God may be politically correct, they say, but don't go so far as to be called a "religious nut."

When Tom was at USC in a course called "Man and Civilization," he was crestfallen to hear his professor ridicule the Bible. When he had finished his diatribe, the professor said, "Anyone who believes in the Bible, stand up."

Tom and one other boy stood to their feet. "Sir, I know in whom I have believed," Tom said. Bless his heart, I was so proud of him. He even quoted part of a verse that he must have memorized during the years my mother nurtured him. The verse is: "Nevertheless I am not ashamed, for I know whom I have believed and am persuaded that He is able to keep what I have committed to Him until that Day" (2 Tim. 1:12).

Paul said that the apostles were "fools for Christ's sake" (1 Cor. 4:10). I have been called a religious crank and fanatic. When I gave my life to Jesus Christ, some people said that it was just a phase I was going through. Well, it's been a forty-eight-year phase, and it will take me out of this life and into the next.

We are called to valor, to a life where we know where we stand and aren't ashamed to proclaim it. Jesus said, "I am the way, the truth, and the life. No one comes to the Father except through Me" (John 14:6). That's that. My life and future life depend on it.

God, Give Us Another Chance

11

> Blessed is the nation whose God is the LORD,
> And the people He has chosen as His own
> inheritance.
>
> Psalm 33:12

I ONCE WROTE, "I believe in my country. I cannot believe that God went to all the trouble of bringing the Pilgrims and other settlers to these shores and guiding the building of the greatest democracy the world has ever seen, only to let it be destroyed."[1]

Is it God's fault that America is following the path to Sodom and Gomorrah? No. He did not invent robots. He fashioned man and woman and gave them freedom to choose. An old hymn of the church says, "On Christ the solid rock, I stand; all other ground is sinking sand." Sometimes I think that America is on quicksand.

Years ago Roy and I rode on horseback down the streets of Philadelphia to Independence Hall. It was on Thanksgiving Day, and I shall never forget the joy on the faces of thousands of free Americans who lined the sidewalks as we passed. What a blessing it is to live in a country that is free!

As we were walking Trigger and Buttermilk through the crowds, I thought of the Declaration of Independence, a document built on the truth of God. I thought of our Founding Fathers who prayed and acted in faith. Whenever I sing, "I'm proud to be an American," I want to remember not to be so proud of our past that I fail to see that we stand in terrible need today to return to God's truth and his values that established our nation.

Which Way, America?

I was jolted recently by a survey taken by George Barna, who heads a research group that mainly assesses church trends. In his findings, based on a nationwide telephone survey of 1,004 adults, ages eighteen and older, the margin of error, Barna said, is plus or minus 3 percentage points. I'm not sharp on mathematics, but that sounds like an accurate kind of survey.

Barna warned that "in view of social trends, the United States faces one of two scenarios in the next five to ten years: moral anarchy or spiritual revival."[2]

People throughout the ages have been told by Jesus that "you are either for me or against me." Fence-sitters must choose one side or the other. If the trend we have seen in the past ten to twenty years of immorality, homosexuality, child abuse, abortion, senseless crimes, lewd language, and all of the other scum we are experiencing today continues, what will our nation be like ten years from now?

Revival or Revulsion?

Some people think that we are on the verge of a spiritual revival unlike anything we have seen since the Great Awakenings of the eighteenth and nineteenth centuries. I look at the phenomenal impact of Promise Keepers, the men's movement started in 1990 when two men, University of Colorado head football coach Bill McCartney and his friend Dr. Dave Wardell, began to pray for an outreach to men. The growth has been astounding, with thousands of men filling some of the largest stadiums in the country to hear about a commitment to Jesus Christ and to their families.

Concerts of Prayer International, Campus Crusade for Christ, the National Day of Prayer, along with small groups of concerned Christians, are growing in numbers as God is raising up people throughout this nation to pray for our country.

Many Christian leaders say they have never seen anything like it. Franklin Graham (Billy's son) said, "The churches believe that everything is coming to a head and that God is moving. Many people in the evangelical community believe that the return of Jesus Christ could be at any moment—and I'm one of those."[3]

Some believe that a spiritual revival will sweep across the land, fulfilling the "Great Commission" to spread the gospel to prepare for the second coming.

Bill Bright, founder of Campus Crusade for Christ, said, "Through the years we've seen the harvest. We've seen tens of millions of people respond to the Gospel. What's happening today has been unprecedented, I'm sure, in all of history. I doubt there has ever been a time like this."[4]

Billy Graham crusades have been growing in number across the world. His physical problems and age have not slowed down the impact of his message.

If morality is down and these positive signs are up, it would seem to me that we have an accelerating war between Satan and Christ for the heart and soul of America.

Out of the Pit

I must admit that when I listen to some of the talk shows where nothing in a person's private life is sacred, when I read of children killing parents and parents molesting children, when I see some of the sleaze the entertainment industry is serving, I want to either scream or throw up. The forces of evil have pulled us so far down into the pit that only widespread repentance and spiritual awakening can lift us out.

A prominent theologian, Erwin Lutzer, said, "There is reason to believe that only a national revival can pull us out of the ditch into which we have slid. I am convinced—as all of us must be—that every human resource is now inadequate and only the direct intervention of God can reverse our spiritual direction."[5]

I agree with Dr. Lutzer. We are always trying to run ahead of God in our desire to make events go our way.

What do we do? Vote for the people we believe best represent God's values? Of course. Roy and I have made public our stand for some politicians. However, I believe that neither a godly president nor leaders who respect the Bible and its principles will be able to reverse the direction of God's judgment.

Revival, as I understand it, means the widespread renewal of the church. The church, however, cannot be revived until individuals are revived. Jesus told Nicodemus that "the wind blows where it wishes" (John 3:8). We are not God's weatherman to discern where or how a revival may take place. But we can look to the past and see what some of the common denominators were in revivals.

What's Happened Before Can Happen Again

In the early 1700s the American churches were suffering from what Christian historians called "creeping paralysis." Into these dry and dead congregations came a powerful preacher, Jonathan Edwards. New life spread from families to churches to towns.

I was excited to find out that while Edwards was preaching, the Lord brought George Whitefield, an Englishman, who was a pioneer in the English revival, to America. Whitefield went on a whirlwind, six-week tour that resulted in the most general awakening the American colonies had experienced. One effect of Whitefield's visits was to rouse the ministers. He said, "The reason why congregations have been so dead is because dead men preach to them."[6]

What was called the "Second Awakening" began in 1857. This is how it happened.

In the middle of the nineteenth century, when our nation was divided over the issue of slavery and people had a selfish, materialistic approach to life, God raised up Jeremiah Lamphier to lead a revival of prayer. In 1857 he began a prayer meeting in the upper room of the Old Fulton Street Dutch Reformed Church in Manhattan. Beginning with only six people, the prayer meeting grew until the church was filled with praying people. By February 1858, nearly ten thousand people a week were being converted. The impact of these prayer meetings spread from city to city across the United States. Cleveland, Detroit, Chicago, Cincinnati—city after city was conquered by the power of believing prayer.[7]

What was the key to these revivals?

1. A time when our nation was in need of values and valor.
2. A few men who were inspired to reach people with the gospel of salvation by faith alone in Christ.
3. Prayer that started at home, spreading to the churches and then to cities.

Ours Is a God of Another Chance

When I was "playing like a Christian," God was patient with me. When I truly repented from my sins, he directed me to a better way of life, a better relationship with those I love, and a better long-term future.

The Bible says: "The Lord is not slack concerning His promise, as some count slackness, but is longsuffering toward us, not willing that any should perish but that all should come to repentance" (2 Peter 3:9).

Isn't that a great promise? He places value on every life. He doesn't discriminate.

When we started this book, I told Carole that I wanted to tell the world where I stand. I am not alone. Thousands throughout America are praying for repentance and revival. Will you join us in this mighty prayer?

"If My people who are called by My name will humble themselves, and pray and seek My face, and turn from their wicked ways, then I will hear from heaven, and will forgive their sin and heal their land" (2 Chron. 7:14). When God speaks about national change (as he did to the nation of Israel in the Old Testament), he speaks to his own people. We are seeing the tide begin to turn today.

The daily news may depress us, but the good news is that God may yet restore America to health.

Roy and I may be in the twilight years of our lives, but I believe this is the most glorious time to be alive!

Notes

Chapter 1: Who Buried America's Values?

1. Peter Marshall and David Manuel, *The Light and the Glory* (Grand Rapids: Revell, 1977), 17.

2. Martin Marty, "The Clamor over Columbus," *Christian History* 11, no. 3, 19.

3. Marshall and Manuel, *The Light and the Glory,* 128.

4. Thomas J. Fleming, *One Small Candle: The Pilgrims' First Year in America* (New York: W.W. Norton, 1963). Quoted in Marshall and Manuel, *The Light and the Glory,* 144.

5. *Christian History* 7, no. 3.

6. Sally Buzbee, "U.S. Students Score Poorly in American History," *Santa Barbara News-Press*, 2 November 1995, p. A3.

Chapter 2: Value of Our American Heritage

1. Marshall and Manuel, *The Light and the Glory,* 285.

2. William J. Federer, *America's God and Country Encyclopedia of Quotations* (Coppell, Tex.: FAME Publishing, 1994), 641.

3. Marshall and Manuel, *The Light and the Glory,* 341.

4. Federer, *America's God and Country,* 648.

5. Marshall and Manuel, *The Light and the Glory,* 343.

6. Federer, *America's God and Country,* 380–83.

Chapter 3: Is Truth Dead?

1. Allan Bloom, *The Closing of the American Mind* (New York: Simon & Schuster, 1987), 25–26.

2. George Barna, *Baby Busters: The Disillusioned Generation* (Chicago: Northfield Publishing, 1994), 66.

3. *Time* (5 October 1992), 34.

4. *Modern Maturity* (November–December 1995), 12.

5. *Bible Society Record* (July–August 1969).

Chapter 5: Value of Tough Times

1. Billy Graham, *Hope for the Troubled Heart* (Waco: Word, 1991), 165.

2. Clebe McClary, *Living Proof* (Pawleys Island, S.C.: Clebe McClary, 1978), 140.

3. Tim Hansel, *You Gotta Keep Dancin'* (Elgin, Ill.: David C. Cook, 1985), 15.

Chapter 6: Family Values in a Fractured World

1. *Victorville Daily Press,* 27 October 1995, p. A7.

2. Daniel Cerone, "Racy Programs Creeping into Family Hour," *Los Angeles Times,* 15 October 1995, p. A28.

3. Ibid.

4. George Barna, "The New American Family," *Moody Monthly* (September 1991), 12.

5. Gigi Graham Tchividjian, *Passing It On* (New York: McCracken Press, 1993), 56.

Chapter 7: Value of Friendships

1. C. H. Spurgeon, *Day by Day,* comp. Al Bryant (Grand Rapids: Kregel, 1980), 89.

2. *Santa Barbara News-Press*, 5 February 1996, p. B1.

3. Dale Evans Rogers, *My Spiritual Diary* (Old Tappan, N.J.: Revell, 1955), 63.

4. Clinton T. Howell, ed., *Lines to Live By* (Nashville: Thomas Nelson, 1972), 103.

Chapter 8: Value of Discipline

1. Eugene H. Peterson, *The Message* (Colorado Springs: NavPress, 1993), 474.

2. Pamela Lopez-Johnson, "Pastor takes a swat at gangs," *Santa Barbara News-Press,* 17 January 1996, p. B1.

3. Ann Landers, "Teach children now or end up with monsters," 10 February 1996.

4. Dale Evans Rogers, *Hear the Children Crying* (Old Tappan, N.J.: Revell, 1978), 54.

5. James Dobson, *Dare to Discipline* (Wheaton: Tyndale House, 1970), 52.

Chapter 9: Value of Patience

1. Oswald Chambers, *My Utmost for His Highest* (Dodd, Mead, 1935), 93.

Chapter 10: A Call to Valor

1. Charles Colson, "Tortured for Christ—and Ignored," *Christianity Today* (March 4, 1996), 80.

2. John Woodbridge, gen. ed., *More Than Conquerors* (Chicago: Moody, 1992), 98.

3. Ibid., 181.

Chapter 11: God, Give Us Another Chance

1. Dale Evans Rogers, *The Woman at the Well* (Old Tappan, N.J.: Revell, 1972), 182.

2. Larry B. Stammer, "Church Attendance Falls to 11-Year Low," *Los Angeles Times*, 6 March 1996, p. B12.

3. Larry B. Stammer, "God Is Up to Something, and It's Big," *Los Angeles Times,* 31 December 1995, p. A1.

4. Ibid.

5. Erwin W. Lutzer, *Will America Be Given Another Chance?* (Chicago: Moody, 1993), 7.

6. *Eerdman's Handbook of Christianity* (Berkhamsted, Herts, England: Lion Publishing, 1977), 434–41.

7. David Jeremiah with C. C. Carlson, *Invasion of Other Gods* (Dallas: Word, 1995), 189.